QUILT CITY COOKBOOK
COMMENTS

"*I* guess this whole dumb thing was my idea. Hadley had about fourteen seconds when she wasn't running the newspaper, running for mayor, quilting, exercising, or solving murders. Not thinking, I said, 'Why don't you put out a cookbook of the goodies you bring to PQQ?' I figured she'd tell me she was too busy, but she said, 'Great idea,' and pulled out her laptop. What's wrong with her?"

— Vivian Franey, fellow member of Paducah Quilters Quorum

"THE WORLD DOESN'T NEED any more cookbooks, but here's another one."

— Jenny Carroll, Hadley's younger sister

"ONCE THAT COCKAMAMIE publisher expressed an interest, there was no stopping Hadley. Her dishes are delicious, and she says I'm her best taster, but I worry about her. It's all too much. And she really should cut back on the coffee."

— Dakota Crowley, Hadley's best friend

. . .

"I'll admit her recipes are scrumptious, and she's funny—I'll grant her that. But enough with the jokes, already. We just want to eat."
— Cindy Baron, PQQ member

"I can't be objective, obviously, so my opinion shouldn't be here, but for some reason it is. Kind of."
— Detective Brandon Green, who has a crush on Hadley

"I'm a quilter, darn it. Probably the best ever, so what do I know about baking?"
— Missy Wendland, widely recognized as the world's worst quilter

"Yes, please. Anything she wants to bake, I'm first, third, and fifth in line. But only if I eat slowly, which ain't likely."
— Garrett Hunt, a private investigator in Paducah, Kentucky

"Let's be honest: It's Hadley's cookbook, but the best recipe in it is mine: the Pucker-Up Lemon Bars. The other stuff's probably okay. I suppose she couldn't put out a cookbook with only one recipe in it, so we get what we get."
— Suzanne Bigelow, McCracken County Attorney

"That's your blurb, Suzanne? Thanks for nothing. I'd hate to receive a condolence card from you: 'Dear Hadley, Thinking of me.'"
— Hadley Carroll, quilter, journalist, solver of murders, cookbook author

QUILT CITY COOKBOOK

RECIPES AND HUMOR BY HADLEY CARROLL

A COMPANION TO THE AWARD-WINNING HADLEY CARROLL MYSTERIES

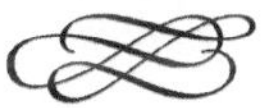

BRUCE LEONARD

Eye-Time
Press

As always, I dedicate this book to Sedonia. You inspire me hourly.
To my mother, Barbara Leonard, who taught me how to bake and
contributed to this cookbook
And to Erminia Dolorosa Veneziale, my maternal grandmother—Dee Dee to
me. Thank you for the laughs, Dee Dee.

CONTENTS

AUTHOR'S NOTE

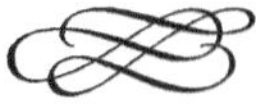

*H*adley Carroll, the quilter, journalist, and narrator of the Hadley Carroll Mysteries, narrates this cookbook.

It contains fictional characters from the series and real-life recipes from my years of co-owning and operating The Blues Bakery, in Ventura, California, as well as recipes, both savory and sweet, that my wife, Sedonia, and I developed for this cookbook.

Readers don't have to have read *Quilt City Murders* or *Quilt City: Panic in Paducah* (or however many novels exist in the series by the time you read this) to appreciate Hadley's intelligence and determination, to sympathize with her troubled childhood, and to realize that she uses humor to attempt to form meaningful human connections.

I, too, am prone to express myself through humor. After all, Hadley and I are similar in many ways. She's a far better quilter than I am, and I envy her weekly gathering of friends during Paducah Quilters Quorum, but I'm married to Sedonia, so I win.

Unlike me, however, Hadley didn't put on weight while she claims to have created many of the recipes that follow. Because I had fun while writing this book, I'll accept my added girth and use it to sustain me while I write the next Hadley Carroll Mystery.

Bon appetit!

GRATEFULLY,
Bruce

THE MUST-READ DISCLAIMER

I, Hadley Carroll, take no responsibility for any accidents you cause or injuries you incur while following the recipes in this cookbook.

Cooking and baking can be dangerous. If you don't know your way around a kitchen and its implements well enough to safely prepare meals without losing a finger, twisting a spine, or burning your house down, then perhaps your time is better spent adult-proofing your home than attempting the following recipes.

If you're inclined to cook while wearing roller skates, bake while drunk, or juggle knives while drunk and on roller skates, well, I'd love to see the videos ... no, that's not what I meant to write.

What I mean is: Please be careful while preparing the following recipes (or disregarding them and calling me names for having the audacity to make my biscuits differently than your Grammy June did).

I only injured myself four times while preparing the following recipes, which I consider an accomplishment because Trapunto likes to sneak up behind me, settle his back one inch from my heels, then wait for me to tumble, preferably with a hot something-or-other in my oven-mitted hands.

He has an ulterior motive, of course, because the food scattered across or splattered on the floor eventually cools, and guess which of us has no problem fishing out a fragment of a peanut butter cookie from beneath the refrigerator, then savoring it? Don't answer that. The question was rhetorical.

Okay, I only did it once, and the five-second rule was in effect, although I'll admit I counted one-Kentucky-Mississippi, two-Kentucky-Mississippi. And, for the record, the fragment was still delicious. And who knew that dog hair added texture?

That last part was a joke, as were the parts before that, as many of the parts hereafter will be. So, if you prefer your cookbooks to be as dry as a martini with neither gin nor vermouth, then perhaps you and I aren't simpatico, so we'll agree not to invite each other to dinner. Or supper, if you prefer. See, we're already bumping heads.

However, if you don't mind laughing while you bake and cook—and won't throw a measuring cup at the refrigerator if I decide now and then to introduce a diversion, similar to this one but perhaps interesting—then we should get along fine.

By the way, I thought about titling this cookbook:

There's No Accounting for Taste.

THE FOOD-PHOTOS DISCLAIMER

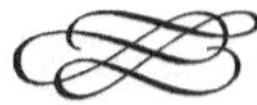

Unlike the photos of the vast majority of food shown in magazines and cookbooks, I used real food without any additives to stage each of the photos within this book.

Food stylists exist. It's a real profession, one that may provide a great deal of satisfaction to its practitioners who help food "pop" in photos. But I shouldn't speculate on their job satisfaction because I've never met a food stylist.

I do know, however, that dye, paint, wax, putty, glue, skewers, and even motor oil are used to enhance what is being presented as food to consumers.

I, however, set the food in the images contained within this cookbook on my counter or table in an arrangement that I thought was appealing, took photos with my phone, then touched-up the photos with the Preview program.

My photos will win no awards, and no one will ooh-and-ahh over them. However, I ate the food in every photograph in this book, something not likely to be true of the food stylists who helped to create those gorgeous images in fancy cookbooks.

THE PALATE DISCLAIMER

*I*f you consider liver and kidneys to be fit for human consumption, then our palates are not aligned, so the following recipes will likely prove to be less wonderful to you than they are to me.

Also, if you feel compelled to add bacon to every dish, including desserts, I can't stop you from doing so. Y'all have purchased this book, so you are free to modify (*ruin!*) the recipes herein in whichever manner you see fit. But when you bring bacon-infused panna cotta to a dinner party, please don't tell them the recipe was derived, even in part, from *Quilt City Cookbook*.

THE MUST-READ INTRODUCTION

When I was a freshman at UCLA, a hunky sophomore named Danny Sullivan asked me if I'd like to drive to Ventura—about an hour and a half away if we drove north on the scenic Pacific Coast Highway and the Ventura Freeway.

"I've never been there," I said, "and you're not giving off any *overt* stalker vibes, so, sure. But why Ventura?"

"A whole-in-the-wall there called The Blues Bakery makes the best peanut butter cookies, lemon bars, and pumpkin muffins in the world." He wore a UCLA sweatshirt, jeans, and penny loafers without socks. He was cute, so I tolerated his socklessness.

"You've sampled the wares from every other bakery on the planet?" I asked.

"I don't have to. You know how they say when you're with the right partner, you'll just know—everything will make sense, and your previous relationships will suddenly embarrass you? That's how extraordinary these baked goods are."

"Wow, that's a heck of an endorsement."

"If after eating there you don't agree with my assessment, I'll give you a hundred bucks. You don't strike me as *overtly* dishonest."

As poor as I was, that sounded like a reasonable proposition because the worst that could happen would be that I'd eat the best baked goods I'd ever eaten.

Well, the worst that could've happened would have been that he was, in fact, a tremendous actor hiding a deep, dark secret in a deep, dark hole, and he felt compelled by forces beyond his control to force me to descend into that hole and immerse myself in his twisted psychosis ... but, wait, that's a different kind of book. This is a cookbook.

The Blues Bakery was on Main Street, under an Oddfellows Lodge, with a white sandwich board adorned with a blue cutout of a guitar on it. The strains of Elmore James's *Dust My Broom* emanated from a speaker facing the street above the door, and the intoxicating scent of peanut-butter brownies tickled my olfactory nerve even before we reached the entrance.

The place was only as wide as a bowling alley, with raw brick walls and a stylized logo of The Blues Bakery painted in white a few feet from the display case, which was stuffed with gorgeous muffins, cookies, lemon bars, and brownies. The muffins were three times the size of an average muffin, and my anxiety flared when I momentarily thought I would have to choose among the dozen kinds of confections.

Luckily, Danny said to the tall, red-headed man behind the counter, "One of each, please."

Bruce Leonard, who owned the bakery with his mother, Barbara Leonard, engaged us in conversation while he filled the order, adding, "The coffees are on me, and I threw in a few extras because you're Bruins, as my mom and I are."

In an attempt to earn myself one hundred dollars, I sampled a peanut butter cookie, a pumpkin muffin, a lemon bar, an oatmeal-raisin cookie, a chocolate chip cookie, a Butternut Beauty, and a Memphis Melody, a sticky mess of pure deliciousness, and a few other sweets I can't remember because apparently consuming a wheelbarrow full of sugar can cause amnesia.

Danny and I sat outside at one of the three small tables in front of the bakery, sipping impeccable Blues Brew coffee and gorging ourselves in a manner befitting a Roman bacchanal. After swallowing the last bite of peanut butter cookie in the name of scientific thoroughness, I said, "You're correct, everything else is the best I've eaten, but I've had better chocolate chip cookies. A check will be fine."

"Nope," he said. "You just acknowledged I won the bet. I never said the chocolate chip cookies were unbeatable."

"Okay, you're right. I was checking to see if sucrose causes forgetfulness in you, too. Thank you for introducing me to The Blues Bakery. I'll definitely return."

"With me?"

"We'll see. How do you feel about quilting?"

* * *

I returned to The Blues Bakery many times and became friendly with Bruce, who eventually shared his recipes with me.

Then, decades later, he created me.

He wanted to write *The Blues Bakery Cookbook* but never found the time while he wrote for and edited magazines or ran newspaper newsrooms. After leaving the last of those newsrooms, he became a novelist, then handed the task of writing this cookbook to me.

If it weren't for *Quilt City Murders*, *Quilt City: Panic in Paducah*, and however many sequels follow, I wouldn't exist, so I wouldn't be able to provide the baked goods every week at Paducah Quilters Quorum, I wouldn't have learned to cook an array of savory dishes, and I wouldn't be able to share the following recipes with you.

Spoiler Alert: I've included Brandon's clams and linguine recipe. Y'all can make of that what you will.

* * *

Unless otherwise specified, when a recipe calls for eggs, I mean large eggs; when it calls for brown sugar, I mean dark brown; when it calls for flour, I mean all-purpose; when it calls for salt, I mean table salt;

and when it calls for olive oil … do I really have to say it? Extra-virgin olive oil only. If we let our standards drop, allowing lesser, adulterated oils to cross our transoms, we'll soon eat our pistachio ice cream slathered in ketchup.

That comparison may seem far-fetched, but go buy a bottle of suspect "olive oil" from one of the forty-three dollar stores in your county, then watch what happens. The slippage won't occur overnight, but in time hot-dogs for breakfast will become a thing. After all, how much difference is there, really, between hot dogs and sausage? Sausage for breakfast is perfectly acceptable to most folks.

But once you allow faux olive oil to cross your transom, you may soon find yourself dipping a hot dog in chocolate sauce and calling it dessert. Don't believe me? Head to a dollar store, then let the culinary catastrophes begin. But don't claim you haven't been warned.

I receive no kickbacks from the extra-virgin olive oil industry, but I just did my best to solicit them.

SWEETS, BAKED GOODS, AND BREAKFAST DESSERTS

AUDREY'S WEDDING COOKIES

*M*akes about 20 cookies

. . .

Audrey Root and I met in the office of *The Daily Bruin* at UCLA during our junior year. She covered the administration, and I covered various aspects of student life, including fraternities and sororities. She'd transferred from UC Santa Barbara after her sophomore year. We hit it off right away when we realized we were equally driven, conscientious, and tenacious.

After graduating, we lost touch as we worked for progressively larger and more well-respected newspapers. However, we reconnected when we both landed at *The Tennessean* in Nashville, before I left to take care of my dying mother.

I'd reached out to Audrey when I'd needed access to *The Tennessean's* database, and she'd told me she'd just gotten engaged. However, I waited for a wedding invitation to arrive but never received one.

One Sunday morning after a bike ride and before church, I called her. Within a few sentences she said, "I've been meaning to call you. I'm sure you've expected an invitation, but Cyrus and I couldn't take the endless advice and bickering. Both families had far too many opinions on how our wedding should be—who should attend, where they should sit, what my dress should look like, what our colors should be, what we should serve, which band we should hire, what the centerpieces should be, where we should go on our honeymoon, how many kids we should have, and what we should name them. Every one of those opinions had at least five options. What should've been one of the best days of our lives was turning into a months-long nightmare.

"One Tuesday evening, Cyrus came home from the office, hugged me, and whispered, 'What are your thoughts on us eloping?' I said, 'I've been wanting to ask you the same thing but thought I'd upset you. I know we'll upset our families, but—' 'But we'll be married, and the marriage is what matters, not the wedding,' he said."

"Congratulations. I'm so happy for you both. Sounds like you made the right decision, and I'm pretty sure if my time ever comes, I'll consider eloping, too."

"Thank you, Hadley. His mom's still very upset at us, refusing even to talk to me, certain that I was responsible for depriving her son of a wedding, despite him telling her at least three times that he broached the subject first and we both agreed to our decision. There's not much I can do. But it's her loss. Eventually, she may forgive us, but until then, she won't get my recipe for Audrey's Wedding Cookies. Or that's what I call them now.

"My mom and I used to make them every Christmas, and she said her mom gave her the basic recipe when she was a girl, but they were called Russian Tea Cakes. Because my great grandmother was from Russia, I'm fine with calling them that, but I get an ironic thrill from naming them Audrey's Wedding Cookies, after having eloped."

When I told her I was writing *Quilt City Cookbook*, she laughed and said, "That's great. If I give it to you, and you include it, I won't give her the recipe if and when she starts acting like an adult: She'll have to buy your book if she wants it." She laughed again.

She said she'd email me the recipe. I thanked her, congratulated her again, told her I was long overdue to meet Cyrus, then made a note to stay in closer touch with her. Nashville's only a little over two hours from Paducah, if traffic cooperates.

With no further ado, I present Audrey's Wedding Cookies.

Preheat oven to 400
1 cup butter (2 sticks), softened
1/2 cup powdered sugar, plus extra to roll the cookies in
2 tsp vanilla extract
1/4 cup milk
2 cups flour
1/8 tsp salt
1 cup chopped pecans

Mix butter, powdered sugar, vanilla until blended. Add milk and blend.

Stir in flour, salt, and pecans (some people prefer walnuts, but some people use burlap for patchwork, so what can we do?), then mix until incorporated.

Form balls the size of a golf ball and set them on a greased cookie sheet.

Bake at 400 for 12 minutes

Let the cookies cool enough for you to pick them up without injury. While the cookies are still warm, roll each in a bowl of powdered sugar.

Let the cookies cool on a baking rack.

Roll the room-temperature cookies through the powdered sugar again.

Yeah, right. As if that's even possible. If these cookies make it to room temperature before disappearing, you either live alone, baked them after eating a large meal, or have used walnuts.

I couldn't help myself. Sorry.

BAKE-YOUR-OWN BISCUITS

*I*f you think politics are divisive in this country, try telling someone how to make biscuits—or how not to.

The following exchange is a close approximation of one that took place during Paducah Quilters Quorum two years ago. We've repaired the damage since.

Please note that I wasn't foolish enough to open my mouth in the middle of a discussion about biscuits.

"Mamma told me early, 'Cindy, never—and I mean *never*—use a mix. Bisquick is for others, and by that I mean losers. And we Baron's are winners!'"

"Maybe so, but *you* don't use lard," Vivian said. "You may not use Bisquick, but you ain't using lard, neither. Whatever you're making, they ain't biscuits."

"Lard? You can use all the lard you want," Evelyn said, "but if you don't use buttermilk—and I've tasted what you call biscuits, bless your heart—you're making something maybe a drunk Yankee might eat."

Dakota chimed in with, "Y'all do what you're gonna do, but if you're not using soft wheat flour, you can add all the lard, buttermilk, Bisquick, bacon, or Maker's Mark you want, but I won't be eating what you're serving."

Donna said, "I'm willing to bet y'all won't agree, but I use Crisco—"

"Get out!" shouted Cindy.

"What?" Donna asked.

"Get out of my home this minute. I mean it!"

"Now, Cindy, she don't know no better," Vivian said. "She's from Philly."

"If you don't get out right now, you're gonna see the opposite of Southern charm, and I guarantee it'll leave a mark."

* * *

IN OTHER WORDS, y'all are going to make biscuits the way you're going to make biscuits, so I'm not foolish enough to subvert tradition, correct your culinary mistakes, or try to protect the palates of others by telling you how real biscuits should be made.

Good luck.

BEST-EVER PEANUT BUTTER COOKIES

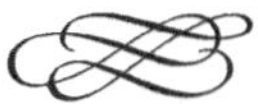

Makes 20 enormous cookies

· · ·

Marriages have broken up over less-significant issues than smooth vs. crunchy peanut butter. Sure, debates about how to spend the family's money, how to raise the kids, and whether toilet paper should drape from the top of the roll or hang from the bottom are more likely to lead to divorce, but very few issues speak more loudly about who we are, what we aspire to, and how we view the universe than smooth vs. crunchy.

You've purchased this book, and I'm neither in a position to grant you a refund if you inexplicably prefer smooth to crunchy, nor am I inclined to do so (because you prefer smooth to crunchy). You may feel that my hard-and-fast preference for crunchy speaks to a certain rigidity in my personality, and you may have a point.

But here's what I'm going to do: I'll look the other way while you replace the correct peanut butter with the inferior, homogenous kind if you promise not to let anyone know where you got this recipe.

Who am I kidding? Use either smooth or crunchy, but follow the recipe otherwise, and the cookies will likely be the best of their kind you've eaten.

If they're not, well, no wonder—you used the wrong peanut butter!

Preheat oven to 375

1 cup CRUNCHY peanut butter (not the natural kind you have to stir)

1 cup Crisco

1 cup sugar, plus more to sprinkle on top

1 cup brown sugar

1 tsp vanilla

2 eggs

1/2 tsp salt

1/2 TBL baking soda

2 cups flour

. . .

CRACK the two eggs in a large mixing bowl, then add peanut butter, Crisco, sugar, brown sugar, and vanilla.

Cream, then add salt, baking soda, and flour.

Mix until incorporated.

Use quality cooking sheets.

Trust me on this. When I was in college and I attempted to make these cookies a week after having scarfed them down at The Blues Bakery, I used the cookie sheets I'd purchased at a Salvation Army for a nickel apiece. One pan buckled, nearly folding in half, and the cookies on the other sprang into flames. The fire extinguisher rendered the entire batch garbage, the landlord was not overly fond of the smoke damage on the ceiling, and the guy I was dating, Danny Sullivan, dumped me because earlier that day I'd somehow managed to cut myself while opening a pack of gum, and he decided, as I doused the final flames, that he feared for his well-being more than he cared for me.

So, again, use good pans. They could save your relationship.

Onto those good pans, scoop golf ball–sized hunks of crunchy goodness. I prefer to line my sheets with Amazon Basics silicone baking sheets. Whether I do this out of a subconscious fear of replicating the flaming cookies of yesteryear or to solicit a sponsorship deal from Amazon, I'll let you be the judge.

I put twelve balls per sheet, spaced in four rows of three, to allow room for the cookies to spread. On occasion, if I've been too generous (perhaps I should say aggressive) with the proportion of the scoop size, the cookies have run together, becoming giant squares, similar to Wendy's hamburgers, but without gristle.

Use a fork to make a crosshatch pattern across each cookie (push down in one direction, rotate the fork ninety degrees, then push down again). After you've scored the cookies, sprinkle some sugar atop each of them. The word "some" is not a technical term; in fact, it's imprecise; these are your cookies, so you can go as wild as you'd like. I pinch as much as I can between my thumb and first three fingers, then gently rub my fingers together above each cookie, sprinkling "some" sugar as I move down the line. Then I replenish my pinch.

Bake for a total of sixteen and a half minutes if you like the bottoms to be slightly darker than golden brown (and you've used quality pans. If your pans are junk, check the cookies much sooner). If you prefer your cookies to be lighter, bake them for about fifteen minutes, remembering, with whichever duration you choose, to rotate the pans between baking racks halfway through so all of the cookies bake evenly.

You are free to eat your cookies however you see fit, obviously, but I am prone to let each bite melt in my mouth, savoring the flavor as the confection dissolves on my tongue. If that's too much information for you, don't read the previous sentence. If you're able to do that after you've read it, you should take that act on the road. You could earn yourself a pretty penny.

But not much more than that.

But if you take along enough of these cookies, you'll make plenty of friends.

Straight-forward recipe:

Preheat oven to 375

1 cup CRUNCHY peanut butter (not the natural kind you have to stir)

1 cup Crisco

1 cup sugar, plus more to sprinkle on top

1 cup brown sugar

1 tsp vanilla

2 eggs

1/2 tsp salt

1/2 TBL baking soda

2 cups flour

Crack the two eggs in a large mixing bowl, then add peanut butter, Crisco, sugar, brown sugar, and vanilla.

Cream, then add salt, baking soda, and flour.

Mix until incorporated.

Scoop into balls the size of golf balls.

Use a fork to make a crosshatch pattern across each cookie.

Sprinkle each cookie with sugar.

Bake for seven minutes at 375, then rotate pans vertically in the oven.

Then bake for eight more minutes.

If you prefer the bottoms to be darker than golden brown, as I do, bake for a total of sixteen and a half minutes on quality baking sheets.

BINGE-WORTHY PECAN BISCOTTI

*M*akes about 24

. . .

I CONSIDER MYSELF PART ITALIAN, although my only basis for this assessment is that I make a great olive-oil cake and a better-than-average lasagna. Of course, I understand that Italians aren't the only nationality that use olive oil, and I know that making a particular meal well isn't dependent on anyone's genetics or heritage. After all, I make excellent lemon bars, but that doesn't make me part citrus.

That joke will probably get me cancelled by Big Citrus. So be it. I may soon have to buy lemons and limes in dark alleys from scofflaw farm workers, but such is the price of comedy—even if the jokes are groan-worthy.

My mom used to say she was "Irish through and through," and her surname, Carroll, supports her claim. It derives from Gaelic and means "fierce in battle." Unfortunately, she was actually "fierce in bottle," but that's a story for another book. She claims she married a man with the same last name, Denton Carroll, my supposed progenitor, not to say father. But the slot on my official birth certificate that should say my father's name is blank.

In other words, I don't know for sure that I'm *not* part Italian.

No, I'm not culturally appropriating biscotti. In fact, many Italians would likely scoff at the recipe below (before you cancel me, I'm not saying that Italians are any more prone to scoff than any other nationality—although I'm not saying they're not, either). Of course, it's safer these days not to say anything at all.

But those of you who know me know I don't do silence. Stewing, mulling, tossing-and-turning, and perseverating—sure, but only in preparation for me to express myself. So, in the name of doing just that—and to enable you to please your friends and family with delightful cookies—I give you Binge-worthy Pecan Biscotti.

PREHEAT OVEN **to 350**
   7 TBLs butter, softened
   2/3 cup sugar
   4 tsp vanilla
   2 tsp baking powder

2 eggs
2 1/4 cups flour
1 cup pecans, diced
Sugar and cinnamon for sprinkling

Lightly grease a large baking sheet.

In a large mixing bowl, combine the butter, sugar, vanilla, and baking powder. Mix until incorporated.

Add the eggs, then mix.

Add the flour, then mix.

Add the pecans, then mix.

If you don't like pecans and would like to make Binge-Worthy Vanilla Biscotti, don't add the pecans, then proceed as you would have.

The dough will probably be wetter than you anticipate, unless you anticipate cookie soup, in which case this is not the cookbook for you. But you may want to write your own cookbook because your culinary ideas are, let's say, unusual. Do what you have to do, although I promise not to buy your cookbook.

Divide the dough in half, then shape into logs about 12 inches long, 2 inches wide, and 3/4 inch thick.

Using a wet spatula, smooth the tops and sides, creating something vaguely resembling a uniform shape.

If you want to sprinkle cinnamon or sugar or—gasp—both onto the logs, now's the time.

Bake at 350 for 25 minutes

Remove from oven.

Reduce oven temperature to 325

Let the logs cool for five minutes. Moisten the tops and sides of the logs with a spatula repeatedly dipped in water or with a spray bottle, preferably filled with water (introducing Maker's Mark at this stage probably wouldn't be unprecedented, although I'm not suggesting you do so).

Slice the logs into cookies with a sharp knife (unless you're going for biscotti crumbles, which aren't a thing, but maybe they should be), about three-quarters of an inch wide. If you have a rebellious streak or a flare for geometry, slice the logs on the diagonal, making fewer, longer cookies that will taste identical to cookies sliced at 90-degree angles. Trust me.

Separate the cookies a little.

Bake at 325 for 25 minutes

Let cool, then do your best to share the biscotti with others. The above recipe is not meant to feed one person. On the other hand, biscotti do not go stale nearly as fast as other homemade cookies do, so if you eat a few here, eat a few there, then eat a few more than a few when you get up to stretch your legs between shows or quilting sessions, who am I to tell you what you should do with your baked goods?

If you want to melt chocolate, then dip the cookies in them, feel free. If you prefer to use a different kind of nut—pistachios taste delicious, unless you're allergic to pistachios. Well, they may still taste delicious, but unless you're a masochist or very quick with an EpiPen, you should probably stick to pecans.

STRAIGHT-FORWARD RECIPE:

   Preheat oven to 350

   7 TBLs butter, softened

   2/3 cup sugar

   4 tsp vanilla

   2 tsp baking powder

   2 eggs

   2 1/4 cups flour

   1 cup pecans, diced

   Sugar and cinnamon for sprinkling

   Lightly grease a large baking sheet.

In a large mixing bowl, combine the butter, sugar, vanilla, and baking powder. Mix until incorporated.

   Add the eggs, then mix.

   Add the flour, then mix.

   Add the pecans, then mix.

Divide the dough in half, then shape into logs about 12 inches long, 2 inches wide, and 3/4 inch thick.

Using a wet spatula, smooth the tops and sides, creating something vaguely resembling a uniform shape.

If you want to sprinkle cinnamon or sugar or both onto the logs, now's the time.

Bake at 350 for 25 minutes

Remove from oven.

Reduce oven temperature to 325

Let the logs cool for five minutes. Moisten the tops and sides of the logs with a spatula repeatedly dipped in water or with a spray bottle, preferably filled with water.

Slice the logs into cookies with a sharp knife, about three-quarters of an inch wide. Separate the cookies a little.

Bake at 325 for 25 minutes

BREAKFAST BROWNIES

*M*akes one 9x13-inch pan
How many servings? How hungry are you?

· · ·

ELLEN CARROLL, our departed mother, frequently left my sister, Jenny, and me alone for days at a time (Mrs. V's Stuffed Shells for more details). Her absences adversely affected us in ways we are still learning (thank you, therapy).

Recently, we found out where she went during some of her unannounced disappearances, and the new information failed to improve how Jenny and I felt about ourselves. In fact, the information threw us backward in ways that readers may learn about in the third Hadley Carroll Mystery, the working title of which is: *Quilt City: Buried Chances*. The title may change because the creative process is nothing if not capricious.

This, however, is a cookbook, so I'll only explain the genesis of the following brownie recipe, not the depth of Jenny's and my psychic wounds.

When I was nine and Jenny seven, our mom didn't return from a trip to Kroger. She was supposed to be buying bread, milk, cereal, eggs, and peanut butter and jelly. Our diet consisted of little else. She almost never purchased vegetables other than potatoes and carrots. Apples and oranges were the only fruits I remember eating until the age of six. I ate my first grapes at a birthday party.

When she didn't return within two hours (the Kroger wasn't far from our horrible apartment building), we suspected she'd gone on another of what Jenny called "Mommy's special adventures." After four hours, we were certain we'd have to fend for ourselves, which, in a certain light, can be seen as "building character," "teaching self-determination," and "creating strong, independent children."

However, the law considers such behavior to be criminal neglect.

We ate stale Saltines and shared the last heel of Wonder bread for dinner.

In the morning, I once again decided not to tip off our neighbors to Mom's disappearance (a few of them must have known what was going on because we'd occasionally find casseroles on our welcome mat). I checked to see if a neighbor had taken pity on us that morning, but no such luck.

I climbed onto the kitchen counter to see if any food was out of sight on the top shelf. I saw a red box of Duncan Hines Milk Chocolate Brownie Mix that I couldn't see when I stood on the floor.

"Yes," I said. I tossed the box to Jenny, who said, "Yippee," when she saw what she'd caught. I climbed down, then realized that we didn't have the vegetable oil or the eggs that the recipe called for. However, during the hundreds of hours I'd spent reading in the McCracken County Public Library, I'd read more than a few cookbooks, so I did what I'd learned to do at age four: I winged it.

I replaced the oil with the last hunk of butter in the fridge, and replaced the eggs with water. Or maybe I did the opposite. Either way, I used a wooden spoon to stir the mix, the butter (which I'd failed to melt), and the water together. I shoved the gloopy mess into a casserole dish that one of the neighbors who'd left us a pity meal had apparently donated to us, then watched the clock until the alarm I'd set went off.

While the brownies cooled, I told Jenny to get dressed for school because we had to eat quickly if we were going to catch the bus.

I'd failed to spray or grease the casserole dish, so Jenny and I scraped the hot, lumpy mess out with spoons.

We ate half of the pan, then hustled to the bus stop.

To our surprise, the brownies proved to be an adequate dinner, too.

The next morning, I found a large casserole dish filled with lasagna on our doorstep with a note that said, "Already cooked. Just need to heat it."

The lasagna got us through the weekend (we ate it cold after I heated it the first time), and Mom showed up at 7 Monday morning with the groceries she'd set out to purchase on Thursday evening.

"Don't dawdle now, but I got you the cereal you like," she said, setting the groceries on the kitchen table. She pulled two bottles of generic bourbon from the paper sack and carried them to her bedroom. I pulled out the box of Kix. Jenny shook her head but knew better than to tell Mom that we didn't like Kix. Did anyone?

A few months later, I made Duncan Hines brownies with the proper ingredients and liked them. Over the years I modified the recipe, eventually starting from scratch. When I decided to introduce peanut butter, my world and worldview improved dramatically.

I present to you the recipe that owes its existence to one of Ellen Carroll's many disappearances.

PREHEAT OVEN to 350
2 sticks of butter, melted
1 1/2 cups of sugar
1 TBL vanilla extract
4 eggs
3/4 cups cocoa
8 ounces of chocolate, melted
1 1/4 cups flour
1/2 teaspoon baking powder
1/4 tsp salt
At least one cup of peanut butter (crunchy preferred, but do what you must)

SPRAY a 9 x 13-inch pan with non-stick spray or smear the pan with butter, coat the butter with flour, then tap the pan and invert it to remove the excess flour.

Using the double-boiler method (or a microwave if you must), melt the chocolate.

While the chocolate is melting, beat the butter, sugar, and vanilla extract in a large mixing bowl until smooth.

Add the eggs, one at a time, mixing the batter between each addition.

Add the flour, baking soda, and salt, then mix until fully incorporated.

Using a spatula, a wooden spoon, or whichever utensil you believe will get the job done, slice ribbons of peanut butter into the batter. Neither rhyme nor reason is required to accomplish this goal. Improvise. Make a peanut-butter smiley face. Or apply meticulousness to the process to ensure that each bite of brownie will contain the same amount of peanut butter.

I don't take the peanut-butter distribution as seriously as I do the consumption of the brownies.

Bake at 350 for 34 minutes or until a toothpick inserted in the middle comes out dry.

Slice the cooled brownies into however many brownies you deem appropriate.

Or do as Jenny and I did long ago and scoop up the deliciousness with spoons. Well, she and I scooped up barely edible gloop, but your baking experience should be significantly more delicious than ours was—now that you own this recipe.

BUTTERNUT BEAUTIES

*M*akes about 25 cookies

DAKOTA'S second cousin once removed and twice incarcerated has nothing to do with this recipe, except that he once ate twenty of the twenty-five cookies I'd baked for a Paducah Quilters Quorum session. I'd left them at Dakota's house a day early because I knew I wouldn't have time to bake on Sunday morning before our session because I had a cycling date with a guy named John John. Thankfully, his last name wasn't Johnson, but I'd have preferred a guy named John John Johnson to the real John John Lee—a lecherous caveman who made inappropriate comments about every woman we passed (at least the comments were inappropriate to me; to him, they were hilarious).

While I was at home showering and trying to erase all memories of John John, Dakota's second cousin once removed was eating the Butternut Beauties I'd left on her kitchen counter as though he was in an eating contest against Joey Chestnut. Upon my arrival, Dakota greeted me with a forlorn expression and said, "He's gone, I promise you, but my creep of a cousin ate nearly all of your cookies."

"Really? How many are left?"

"Five. Well, four. I ate mine." She smiled.

"How was it?"

"Amazing."

"If your kitchen's well-stocked, I'll whip up another batch."

"If my kitchen were well-stocked, it wouldn't be my kitchen." She owned as many high-end appliances, pots and pans, and utensils as her huge kitchen could hold, but she almost never cooked, so she almost never had a well-stocked pantry or a refrigerator filled with much more than takeout left-overs.

The other members of PQQ shared the remaining four cookies, which was fine by me because I'd left two for myself at home.

. . .

1 STICK BUTTER, softened (1/4 pound. If you prefer grams, please use a search engine of your choice to make the conversion because if I list grams here, inevitably some baker will use that measurement, and the cookies will be rejected even by the dog, and they were meant for the work meeting tomorrow, and now there's no time to bake another batch, so who else is there to blame but the author?)

1/2 stick Crisco (1/2 cup) or another brand of shortening if you don't care how the cookies turn out

½ **cup sugar**

½ **tsp vanilla**

1 TBL water

¾ **cup pecans or almonds**, or feel free to use a different kind of nut, but I can't vouch for the results.

1 ¾ cups all-purpose flour

Preheat oven to **350 degrees Fahrenheit** (see the explanation above for why I haven't included the Celsius temperature).

In a medium-sized mixing bowl, cream the butter, Crisco, sugar, and vanilla.

In a Cuisinart, or a thrift-store food processor that has lost its shine but keeps chugging along (sound familiar?), finely chop the pecans, almonds, or other questionable nut choice. Fine means fine, so don't rush this part. Have an adult beverage while the nuts obliterate. No, maybe you shouldn't. There's a whirling blade only inches away, and I don't know your tolerance for alcohol or the length of your fingers, so forget I mentioned it.

Add the pulverized nuts to the butter mixture, then, without creaming the nuts and butter first, add 1 ¾ cups of flour.

Mix until incorporated.

Using a tablespoon or a soup spoon (but never chopsticks), scoop a dollop somewhere between the size of a Barn Swallow's egg and a golf ball.

On two cookie sheets, place the 25 or so cookies (depends on the size of each, obviously. Go for one big one, if you like, which would eliminate the confusion caused by those pesky Barn Swallows' eggs).

Using a teaspoon or your thumb (*You did wash your hands before you started all this, didn't you?*), form a dimple, a dent, or an indentation in the top of each cookie.

Actually, they're not cookies yet—they're just dough, delicious though they may be. Sure, we've all been told not to eat raw dough, but we've also been told not to write long digressions in the middle of recipes, yet who among us, after drinking while using a Cuisinart, hasn't rambled …

Never mind, but if you feel compelled to sample the dough now to see if it's safe to put in the oven, you would be in excellent company. I do, however, suggest that you do not eat four … okay, five … unbaked Butternut Beauties before you bake them. Trust me.

Bake for 14 minutes, preferably alternating the pans vertically in your oven at seven minutes so both pans receive the same amount of heat. If your oven is large enough to accommodate both pans side by side, then maybe I should attend Thanksgiving at your house because your kitchen sounds awesome, and Thanksgiving is my favorite holiday. I'll bring the Butternut Beauties.

As difficult as this step will be, do your best to let the cookies cool before you add a blurp of jelly, preferably raspberry, to the indentation. If you think blurp isn't a word, then why did you just read it in a recipe?

In truth, I think the jelly is gilding the lily, but many people have a higher tolerance for sugar than I do (my constitution changed after that first visit to The Blues Bakery. Now every time I think about eating an entire display case full of baked goods, I shudder, then go for a run). If you prefer your Butternut Beauties jellied, then I hope you enjoy them. And share them.

BLUESBERRY MUFFINS

*M*akes about a dozen

. . .

THE FIRST TIME I walked into The Blues Bakery I laughed at how small it was. I could touch both walls of what would have been a hallway in another business, but in that establishment *was* the establishment, other than the slightly wider section in the back where the employees did the baking. That section was about the size of a decent walk-in closet in a mediocre apartment complex in a sketchy neighborhood.

And yet when I tasted the baked goods, I wondered why other bakeries didn't squeeze into tighter quarters because The Blues Bakery produced exceptional baked goods, and who was I to say that the confining quarters didn't play a role?

Nearly every home baker has made blueberry muffins, to better or worse effect. I'm not saying this is the only difference—but it could be the primary difference: The blueberry muffins at The Blues Bakery were called Bluesberry Muffins, so, again, perhaps the S contributes to their deliciousness.

Of course, I'm kidding, because Bruce shared the formula with me. By the way, baking recipes should really be called formulas, and they are in many bakeries, because unlike in savory dishes in which a pinch of this or a dash of that can affect the taste but won't likely make a dish go splat, too much flour or not enough baking powder, for example, in a baking formula can result in a frustrated baker having to throw out the gloopy mess that never rose, wasting time and money and requiring a second effort. And occasionally a third.

Despite knowing that it is better to under promise and over deliver, I've risked doing the opposite by singing the praises of the scrumptious muffins that result from the following formula. I'm a risk taker. I can't help it.

PREHEAT OVEN **to 350**
 1 1/2 sticks butter (3/4 or a cup), melted, then cooled
 3 eggs
 1 1/4 cups sugar
 1/2 tsp vanilla
 1 1/8 cups low-fat buttermilk

1/2 tsp salt
2 TBLs baking powder
3 1/2 cups flour
1 1/4 cups frozen blueberries
Crack three eggs into a large, empty mixing bowl.
Add sugar, vanilla, and cooled butter.
Cream.
Add buttermilk, then mix.
Add salt, baking powder, and flour.
Mix until incorporated.

Add bluesberries, then fold into batter gently, unless you want violet muffins (let's all admit it together: blueberries and bluesberries aren't blue. They're closer to purple. In order to prevent an etymological and semantic debate, we can agree to call the color blue, but would calling them purpleberries have killed anyone?).

Line the muffin tins with paper muffin cups, or grease them, flour them, and remove the excess flour, then scoop with whichever utensil pleases you (if you choose a fork, perhaps you should take up drawing, instead), until the cups are between heaping and overflowing.

Bake at 350 for 32 minutes. If you're unsure (and, lets' face it, we all are from time to time, and many of us are all the time), insert a toothpick into a muffin. If it comes out dry, then let them cool, then dig in. If it's wet, leave the muffins in for another minute or two.

Start saying bluesberry in public just to gauge people's reactions.

CHOCOLATE CHIP COOKIES FOR ADULTS

*M*akes 18-20

. . .

THE STORY behind this cookie goes like this: I was stuck behind enemy lines with a double agent named Jodie or Jackie, which I would have found confusing, but I wasn't the double agent, so names weren't foremost on my mind. What filled my head were concerns about how we were going to blow the bridge in the next forty seconds before the train arrived without the enemies on either side of us exposing our position first, thus ending our campaign.

I looked toward Jodie/Jackie, who wasn't fully engaged in our mission, and I knew we were in trouble. When she twirled her hair and said, "Hadley Gladly, this game isn't fun, and I want a cookie," I knew our mission had gone bust, so I took Jenny inside and pulled out the ingredients to make Nestlé Toll House Chocolate Chip Cookies.

Most of us likely grew up eating some variation on this classic, and if you're still a Toll House gal or guy, so be it. After baking a batch that afternoon for Jenny and me, and then using the same recipe a couple dozen more times, I started to think the cookies were too sweet, almost one-note. Oodles of sugar combined with two cups of chocolate chips (the recipe, written by a company in the business of selling chocolate chips—as well as umpteen other products—comes on the bag of chocolate chips, so us using too many chocolate chips is in the company's best interest, not necessarily ours or the cookies').

So, I started to tinker, and eventually I came up with the following recipe, which delivers chocolate chip cookies evocative of our childhoods but without the all-sugar-all-the-time agenda of childhood.

PREHEAT OVEN **to 375**
    1 cup Crisco
    1/2 cup sugar
    1/2 cup brown sugar
    2 eggs
    2 tsps vanilla
    1/2 tsp salt
    One scant tsp baking soda
    2 1/4 cups flour

1 cup semi-sweet chocolate chips
1 cup chopped walnuts, optional

COMBINE THE EGGS, Crisco, sugar, brown sugar, and vanilla in a large mixing bowl.

Cream, then add salt, baking soda, and flour.

Mix until incorporated, then add chocolate chips and walnuts, if using them, and mix. If not incorporating walnuts, well, there's not a thing I can do to convince you otherwise, and I won't bother to try because you know what you like, and, let's face it, many of you went straight to your cupboards and pulled out the ingredients to make Toll House Chocolate Chip Cookies exactly as laid out on the package as soon as I mentioned them, so who am I to attempt to influence you?

Scoop golf-ball sized balls of dough onto cookie sheets (I use Amazon Basics silicone sheets on my trays because I like the way they brown the bottoms and shorten the baking time a smidge).

Because you'll likely use two cookie sheets (unless you have a commercial oven and are using a full sheet), you should rotate the trays vertically at the halfway mark.

Bake for seven and a half minutes, rotate, then seven and a half minutes more (fifteen minutes total, for those too tired or hungry to add).

Let cool before consuming them, unless you like tongue blisters.

CINNAMON PINEAPPLE UPSIDE-DOWN CAKE

S erves 10 or 12 humans or one grizzly bear

. . .

WHEN JAKE SMITH, a page designer for the *Paducah Chronicle*, learned I was writing a cookbook, he said to me, "I don't know if you're looking for recipes, but I have one my great granddaddy gave to me, and it's pretty darned good."

"What kind of recipe?"

"Oh, sorry. Pineapple upside-down cake, but Grandpop called it cinnamon pineapple upside-down cake because he punched it up."

"Sounds great." He pulled a piece of copy paper from his backpack and handed it to me. I read it and said, "Looks excellent. I'll try it. If it tastes good enough to make the cut, I'll include it and give you and your great grandfather credit for providing it."

"That's wonderful. It has kind of an interesting story. Grandpop grew up on the South Side and never saw a pineapple until he was stationed on the U.S.S. West Virginia in Pearl Harbor when it was attacked on Dec. 7. Told me he became a man that day and made him realize every day thereafter was a gift he was lucky to receive.

"He served in the mess with the hero Dorie Miller. Grandpop said he wished he'd had the strength of mind to man the guns the way Dorie did, but he said he was fortunate just to get off the ship alive. He was a different man when he got home, he said, so when he asked Nanna, she accepted. He said she never would've if he hadn't grown up the way he did in the Navy. The rest, as they say, is history."

"That's interesting and lucky. You wouldn't exist otherwise."

"No, and I wouldn't be able to pass along the recipe. It was developed by the African Americans in the mess. Grandpop said it was his idea to bump up the cinnamon. And he swapped out butter for olive oil when he got home. Not for sure, but it could've helped him live to 103."

"Or it could have been the pineapples. Whatever it was, he did something right, and I'll be honored to include his recipe. Thank you for giving it to me."

"My pleasure. Enjoy."

PREHEAT OVEN to 350

2 TBLs butter, melted
1/2 cup brown sugar
1 can pineapple slices
2 1/4 cups flour
2 tsps baking powder
1 TBL cinnamon
1/4 tsp salt
1/2 cup olive oil
1 cup sugar
2 eggs
2 tsps vanilla
2/3 cup milk
Cherries are optional

IN A 10-INCH SPRING-FORM PAN, melt the butter in the oven, then carefully swirl the melted butter around the bottom of the pan, being sure to coat it all.

Spread the brown sugar evenly across the pan, covering all of it.

Place one pineapple slice in the middle of the pan and five around the edges. If you want to add a cherry (without pits, unless you're clumsily trying to commit a murder. For the record, the cherries won't do the trick, unless your potential victim is allergic to cherries. Then you may succeed with the murder, but you won't get away with it, not when you're serving this cake at the annual holiday party at work. Too many witnesses. Look, you obviously haven't thought this murder through, so you should just serve the cake, with or without cherries, and enjoy the party. But watch your alcohol intake. Too much, and you could end up doing something stupid—like plan a murder).

In a bowl large enough to contain the following ingredients, combine the flour, baking powder, cinnamon, and salt.

In another bowl, beat the olive oil and the sugar together for longer than feels comfortable.

Add an egg, then beat the mix well. Add the other, then repeat.

Add the vanilla, then mix again.

Pour the dry ingredients into the wet ones. Mix in some of the dry, then add some milk, then some more dry, then some milk, and end with the dry.

Write a limerick that begins with the line: "A baker was halfway to wilting"

Pour the batter into the spring-form pan, spread the batter evenly throughout, then **bake at 350 for 55 minutes**. Test for doneness with a toothpick. Put the toothpick between your teeth, pretend you're in a Western, and say, "Don't want to kill you with a cherry, but I will if I must."

After five minutes of cooling off (both you and the cake), carefully invert the cake, release the pan, and remove the bottom (now top). No matter how absurdly difficult this part sounds, let the cake cool to room temperature before slicing it.

HERE'S MY LIMERICK:
    A baker was halfway to wilting
    Her cake was lopsided and tilting
    She counted to ten
    Surrendered and then
    Decided to do some more quilting

DR. ELAINE BOURGET'S BANANA NUT BREAD

*M*akes 1 gorgeous loaf

I'D CONSIDERED ASKING the psychiatrist who'd helped get me through various crises whether writing a cookbook was good for my mental health. However, because I wanted to write the cookbook, and I didn't want anyone to dissuade me from this pursuit, I didn't dial Dr. Elaine Bourget's number.

However, while I was leaving Café de Fae after eating brunch, I heard someone call my name, and I turned to see Elaine and her husband, Chad, seated on the front porch. She introduced me to Chad, and vice versa, and asked me what I was up to.

"I did something I almost certainly shouldn't have done," I said. "I took on another project."

"It's good to keep busy, but, yes, you tend to overdo it," she said. "What's the project?"

"I'm writing a cookbook. My fellow PQQers convinced me I should share the goodies I make for them each week with the world, or at least the sliver of the world that exists in and around Paducah."

"Doesn't sound like a bad idea. The lemon bar you gave me was the best ever. And you're being self-negating. The internet is global, so if you put out an ebook, people far outside the Purchase Region will be able to indulge in your specialties."

"Well, most of them aren't really mine. They were given to me by the former owner of The Blues Bakery, and many of them come from friends and fellow quilters."

"But you're writing the cookbook, so give credit where credit's due. And if you don't already have a recipe for banana nut bread, I'll email you the one my sister and I modified from one of our grandmother's recipes."

"That would be excellent. Thank you very much."

"If it all begins to feel like too much, you know how to reach me."

"I do. Thank you, and nice to meet you, Chad."

"Nice to meet you, too, Hadley. I'd like to be the first to buy your cookbook. Where can I buy it?"

"Contributors will receive free copies, so I won't take your money, but thank you for the offer."

PREHEAT OVEN **to 350**

    1/4 pound butter, melted

    11 ounces over-ripe bananas (about 3 medium bananas)

    3 eggs, beaten

    1 cup sugar

    5 ounces plain yogurt

1 tsp baking powder
1 tsp baking soda
1 tsp cinnamon
2 cups flour
1 cup walnuts, chopped

Spray with non-stick spray or use the butter-and-flour method on a loaf pan.

Mash the bananas in a large mixing bowl, add the melted butter, then mix.

Add the eggs, sugar, and yogurt, then mix.

Add the baking powder, baking soda, cinnamon, and flour, then mix.

Add the chopped walnuts, then mix.

Pour into the pan and bake for … this is where it gets tricky.

What is your loaf pan made of and how large is it?

My glass loaf pan is very wide and deep, so it takes a whopping 80 minutes for the loaf to bake through.

If your loaf pan is long and thin, then you should probably begin checking for doneness at 60 or 65 minutes.

I've pulled the loaf out at 75 minutes, convinced that it was baked thoroughly, only to find that the bottom half an inch wasn't baked through. The rest was still delicious, and I told myself that I hadn't eaten an entire loaf of banana nut bread by myself because I left that bottom half inch—okay, maybe quarter-inch—uneaten.

Society doesn't celebrate the ability to rationalize as it should.

DUTCH BOUNTY

. . .

CALLING A DISH THAT WE EAT A "BABY" seems wrong. I know that in today's climate we're not supposed to judge other people's proclivities, but I almost always draw the line at cannibalism.

Therefore, I'm not calling the following recipe a Dutch Baby, as the pancake-like dish is called, at least in America.

Residents of the Netherlands don't likely refer to their offspring as food, so I'm rebranding this dish that can be tinkered with to create a savory meal (add cheese, bacon, or a side of beef) or a variety of breakfast options (strawberries, peanut butter, chocolate).

I present to you Dutch Bounty, a meal that should cause only vegans to feel squeamish.

3 TBLs butter

3 eggs, preferably at room temperature, but who has that kind of patience?

1/2 cup heavy cream (or milk, if you prefer inferior meals)

5/8 cup flour (you didn't think there'd be math, did you?)

1 TBL sugar

1 tsp cinnamon

2 tsps vanilla extract

PUT the butter in a deep 8-inch cast-iron skillet.

A larger one will work, but the climb up the sides will be less impressive. And a pan made from something other than cast-iron will probably work, although I don't guarantee that.

Actually, I don't guarantee anything in this book. That would imply a legal contract that doesn't exist between us.

Sure, I stand by my dishes and believe many of them are excellent, but guaranteeing that you'll like them? What am I, a moron?

Don't answer that. The question was rhetorical.

PUT the skillet in the oven that you now set to 425.

While the butter melts and the oven gets up to temp, combine all of the other ingredients above in a blender or similar appliance, and whir the heck out of all of it.

When the oven has reached 425, remove the HOT skillet while wearing an oven mitt or two. Swirl the butter so it covers the bottom, then pour the batter into the skillet.

Carefully return the skillet to the oven, then **bake at 425 for 20 minutes**.

If you prefer only to sprinkle powdered sugar on your appropriately named and recently prepared Dutch Bounty, as I do, now's the time to do it.

Or you can top the servings with fruit, if you desire.

If you decide to go the savory route, I suggest cutting down the sugar content above by at least a teaspoon (meaning go from 1 tablespoon to 2 teaspoons, although only using 1 teaspoon is an option, especially if you intend to add brown-sugar-and-maple-glazed bacon. And if you do use bacon, I suggest you also use unsalted butter because the result will be too salty).

You have options, and I have to go eat another serving.

EASIER-THAN-PIE MUFFINS

Makes 8 small muffins

. . .

PADUCAH QUILTERS QUORUM member Janet Loy had long wanted to go to Paris, France, but her smart-aleck husband bought them bus tickets to Paris, Texas, and said, "You're always saying, 'I want to go to Paris. Why can't we go to Paris?' Well, you never said which one."

After he died, Janet flew to France, dined lavishly in various restaurants, cafés, bistros, and patisseries, took a few cooking classes, and fell in love with French Breakfast Puffs (I don't know what they're called in French, but the name probably doesn't sound like a kids' cereal).

When she returned to Paducah, she tinkered with the recipe that a chef wrote for her on a napkin (she said the muffins were delicious but needed a bit of a kick, so she gave them one). She decreased the sugar, increased the cinnamon and nutmeg, and added cloves.

Before I took over dessert duties at PQQ, Janet served us a batch of what she renamed Easier-than-Pie Muffins, and we all wondered why she'd made so few. Her behavior bordered on stinginess, considering how amazing they proved to be.

In other words, if you have an extra muffin tin or two, you may want to make multiples of the following recipe.

By the way, they freeze well, especially if you don't add the topping before you set them in the freezer. When you're ready, let them thaw, add the topping, and try to eat only one muffin at a time.

PREHEAT OVEN to 350
   1/3 cup Crisco
   3/8 cup sugar
   1 egg
   1 1/4 cups flour
   1 1/2 tsps baking powder
   1/2 tsp nutmeg
   1/4 tsp cinnamon
   1/8 tsp cloves
   1/4 tsp salt
   3/8 cup milk

. . .

FOR THE TOPPING:
1/4 cup butter, melted
1/2 cup sugar
1 1/2 tsps cinnamon

IN A MIXING BOWL, cream the Crisco, sugar, and egg.

In a different bowl, mix the flour, baking powder, nutmeg, cinnamon, cloves, and salt.

Add the dry ingredients to the wet a little at a time, introducing the milk between each addition. Mix everything until incorporated.

If you're making the proportions above, spray eight of the twelve muffin cups with non-stick spray or use the butter-then-flour method, which I prefer because I taste the spray occasionally. Depending on the brand, it can taste like the artificial butter that is often served in movie theaters or like an industrial solvent that expired in 1972.

In case you're unaware of the butter-then-flour method: Take a stick of butter (or a smear of it on a napkin, if you'd prefer) and coat the inside of the muffin cups. Sprinkle flour into each cup, and shake the tin so the flour covers all of the butter. Then tap the tin against something firm (preferably not your partner's head), and discard the excess flour.

When you're ready (possibly while wearing a beret), fill each cup about three-quarters full (quick math question: If eight of twelve muffin cups are filled three-quarters full by a a beret-wearing baker once in a twenty-four-hour period during the third quarter of the fiscal year, what color spatula should you use?).

I question the need for this next step (questioning is in my nature), but Janet let me know that she adds a little water to the empty muffin cups, so I add the water while questioning whether I should.

Bake at 350 for 20 minutes

Ovens and muffin tins differ, so check with a toothpick to see if they're fully baked. If the toothpick comes out dry, they're done.

Topping

Melt the butter in one bowl.

Mix the cinnamon and sugar in another

When the muffins are cool enough to touch (trust me, I had to delay my enjoyment of my breakfast dessert after having to apply an ice cube to my index finger and thumb after trying to coax a scalding muffin from its cup), dip them one at a time into the melted butter, then into the cinnamon-sugar mixture.

For the record, I prefer my Easier than Pie Muffins without the topping because cinnamon, sugar, and fat already exist within them.

However, do whatever works for you.

EXCELLENT ESPRESSO CUPCAKES

Makes 6 Texas-tin muffins or 12 regular-sized ones

. . .

You've probably noticed that I'm fond of coffee.

Just as I'm "fond" of quilting and breathing.

Have I been informed by concerned friends and a cardiologist that I should consume fewer cups of coffee than I do (and by cup I mean giant mug or tumbler)? Have these same people sung the praises of decaf? Yes to both questions. How did I respond to their suggestions?

By sticking a finger in each ear and saying loudly, "Na-na-na-na-na-na-na-na-na-na-na-na."

I'm kidding, of course.

About the fingers.

I was wearing earbuds the last time Dakota suggested that my caffeine intake made it seem as though I was trying to levitate, so I turned up the volume and said, "Na-na-na-na-na-na-na-na-na-na-na-na."

Not really. I'm not a toddler.

I only thought about doing these things, then downed another gulp of Starbucks Holiday Blend.

You see where I'm going with this, don't you? You read the name of this recipe, and your momma didn't "raise no fools." Well, your brother, but that wasn't her fault. He snorted sand all by himself, although he claims a pesky neighbor kid dared him. But how can you trust him, with his head full of sand?

Anyway, because I am who I am, I agreed to cut back on the amount of coffee I drink when I realized I could *eat* my coffee.

It's socially acceptable to eat muffins for breakfast, accompanied by coffee. However, I've never seen a menu that lists a breakfast cupcake.

Yes, differences exist between the two: muffins are more dense and less sweet (like your brother), and cupcakes are fluffy and sweet, or at least they should be.

Because I drink my coffee black, I believe I'm entitled to eat breakfast cupcakes—the combination adds up to the same amount of sugar I would consume if I sweetened my coffee and ate a muffin.

Have I done the math above? No, but the argument makes sense if you're already hopped up on caffeine.

Traditionally, cupcakes are frosted, so I frosted one with an espresso-infused buttercream frosting (or icing, if you prefer) so I could use it in the photo. The result was delicious but too sweet for my tastes. Please feel free to frost or ice as you see fit.

I present Excellent Espresso Cupcakes.

PREHEAT OVEN to 320

1 1/2 cups flour

2 TBLs espresso powder (if you balk at the expense, remember that this ingredient is essential to the Magnificent Mocha Panna Cotta, and if you're not going to make that dessert, then why did you buy this cookbook? You've probably been muttering that question under your breath or shouting it often while reading it, especially when I go off on tangents such as this one)

1 1/2 tsps baking powder

1/8 tsp salt

3/4 cup brown sugar

2 tsps milk

2 tsps vanilla extract

3 eggs

MIX THE FLOUR, espresso powder, baking powder, and salt in a large bowl (preferably not the dog's).

Add the brown sugar, milk, and vanilla extract, then mix until incorporated.

Add the eggs one at a time, beating the mixture between each.

Line 6 Texas-tin muffin cups with large cupcake liners or 12 traditional tins with regular liners. Fill the cups with an equal amount of batter unless you're building up an insanity defense for your pending court date.

Bake at 320 for 23 minutes if making the large cupcakes or 15

or so for the small ones. However, check both sizes for doneness with a toothpick before making your final determination.

By the way, it's none of your business how many solid cups of coffee I ate while testing this recipe.

"Na-na-na-na-na-na-na-na-na-na-na-na-na."

EXCEPTIONAL ESPRESSO BISCOTTI

Makes 24 or so

. . .

THIS RECIPE IS identical to the one for Binge-Worthy Pecan Biscotti (although some of the jokes differ), except that instead of adding chopped pecans, you should add 3 teaspoons (which, for the record, equals one tablespoon) of espresso powder at the end, when you would have added the pecans.

By the way, if you leave out the espresso and the pecans, the resulting biscotti—let's call them vanilla biscotti—are exceptional, too.

And the second by the way: This recipe will probably appeal most to people who like dark chocolate, meaning those who like a little bitterness and don't need overt sweetness. For those with a true sweet tooth, I'd suggest bumping the sugar to 3/4 cup, or adding the melted chocolate that I mention in the last step. For the purposes of this paragraph, that should be milk chocolate or semi-sweet. If you're really a fan of dark chocolate, as I am, you can gild the lily by making that last addition dark.

And a third by the way: Someone should start The Gilded Quilt Guild.

PREHEAT OVEN to 350
7 TBLs butter, softened
2/3 cup sugar
4 tsps vanilla
2 tsps baking powder
2 eggs
2 1/4 cups flour
1 TBL espresso powder (that's 3 teaspoons, in case you were wondering)
Sugar for sprinkling

LIGHTLY GREASE A LARGE BAKING SHEET.

In a large mixing bowl, combine the butter, sugar, vanilla, and baking powder. Mix until incorporated.

Add the eggs, then mix.

Add the flour, then mix.

Add the pecans, then mix.

The dough will be wet. It's best to lightly flour your hands and/or the work surface on which you will form the logs.

Divide the dough in half, then shape into logs about 12 inches long, 2 inches wide, and 3/4 inch thick.

Using a wet spatula, smooth the tops and sides, creating something resembling a uniform shape, unless you feel particularly creative today.

If you want to sprinkle sugar onto the logs, now's the time.

Bake at 350 for 25 minutes

Reduce oven temperature to 325

LET the logs cool for five minutes. Moisten the tops and sides of the logs with a spatula repeatedly dipped in water or with a spray bottle, preferably filled with water (if you happen to be an author of mysteries and are thinking about having someone introduce poison to the recipe at this point, don't do so. Turn your own recipe into a weapon, not mine. Liability issues probably exist. Plus, what if Bruce, in a pinch, needed a plot device to propel his next mystery to its surprising, satisfying conclusion, and a spray bottle filled with poison seemed perfect. He would feel like he'd be stealing the idea from you, even though you got the idea from me, and he created me. As you see, it's all very confusing, so just make the darn cookies as specified). Skipping this step will make slicing the log more difficult.

Slice the logs into cookies with a sharp knife (unless you're going for biscotti crumbles, which aren't a thing but maybe should be) about three-quarters of an inch wide. If you have a rebellious streak or a flair for geometry, slice the logs on the diagonal, making fewer, longer cookies that will taste identical to cookies sliced at 90-degree angles. Trust me.

Separate the cookies a little.

Bake at 325 for 25 minutes

Let cool, then do your best to share the biscotti with others. The above recipe is not meant to feed one person. On the other hand, biscotti do not go stale nearly as fast as other homemade cookies do, so if you eat a few here, eat a few there, then eat a few more than a few when you get up to stretch your legs between shows or quilting sessions, who am I to tell you what you should do with your baked creations?

If you want to melt chocolate, then dip the cookies in them, feel free. Doing so may elevate this dessert to heretofore unreached culinary heights, rendering the rest of your life far less special in relation, so unless you want to feel only ho-hum about aspects of your life that used to bring you joy and satisfaction, perhaps you should avoid adding the chocolate. You've been warned.

HILLARY HUNT'S LEMON OLIVE OIL CAKE

Makes a 9-inch cake

How many servings? At least one

. . .

IF YOU'VE READ the cozy mysteries (with an edge) that feature me and my attitude, you know about Garrett Hunt, the former boxer turned private investigator who has assisted me (come to my rescue?) on more than one case.

Garrett is a very large man whose face reveals the scars and broken cartilage he sustained in the ring and the ravages of grief caused by his life. Breast cancer took his wife and one of his daughters from him. Understandably, his worldview darkened after those losses, and he filled the void with alcohol.

Because I understand loss and the dangers of heavy drinking (and because Garrett is a good human being, one who has helped me significantly), we've become friends, in addition to maintaining our professional relationship.

After I'd given him some peanut butter cookies, he returned the favor by bringing me a large slice of lemon olive oil cake that was the best cake I'd ever eaten—not too sweet but tangy, moist, and memorable.

When I'd asked him whose recipe it was, he said, "Hillary's. She created it secretly before our third date because I'd mentioned that when I was a kid I had a slice of olive oil cake at my great aunt's house in Philly, and I've never had a piece of cake I liked as much since.

"Hillary took it upon herself to win my heart by way of my stomach, but, truth be told, I knew I was half-way gone on our first date. By the end of our second, I knew I would be a very bitter man if I managed to blow it with her. Luckily, I didn't. Her cake was just frosting, I guess you could say, because she felt the same way about me. Don't ask me why.

"'Course, I wasn't this ugly and fat way back then, and I've been known to have a thought worth having, and she appreciated the way my mind works, so the rest is history. At least until it all ended.

"But I have to thank you, Hadley, because you let me know that we can endlessly carp about our awful luck, or we can realize we're still here, and we could've been the one who died of cancer, or who was murdered, in Matt's case. So, thanks to you, nowadays I acknowledge I'm able to eat this delicious cake, then express my gratitude. Notice how small your piece is relative to how much I already ate." He laughed hard, which made me feel good.

A few months later when I told him I was writing a cookbook, he offered me Hillary's recipe (I didn't solicit it—I promise). I never knew her, but I'm sure I would have liked her because any woman who would create a recipe from scratch to increase her odds of finding and keeping true love would be a friend of mine.

PREHEAT OVEN to 325
 2 3/4 cups flour
 1/2 tsp salt
 1 1/2 tsps baking soda
 3 eggs, at room temperature
 Zest of three lemons
 1 1/4 cups sugar
 1 cup olive oil
 1/2 cup low-fat milk
 2/3 cup real lemon juice
 2 tsps vanilla
 Powdered sugar for the top

IN A SMALL BOWL, mix the flour, salt, and baking soda.

In a large bowl, beat the eggs for about a minute on the medium setting with a hand mixer.

Add the lemon zest and the sugar, then beat on high for at least two minutes.

Pour in the olive oil while the beaters are on medium speed, and mix until incorporated.

Blend in half of the flour mixture, then add the lemon juice and milk, mixing until incorporated.

Mix in the remaining flour mixture, being sure not to over mix the batter.

Spray a 9-inch spring-form pan with non-stick coating (or use the butter-and-flour method).

Pour the batter into the pan, then **bake at 325 for 60 minutes**. Check for doneness with a toothpick. At 62 minutes, my cake came out better than I hoped it would, and I had high hopes.

Sift powdered sugar on top.

Let it cool if you care how the slices look. If not, dig in.

Invite your friends over. Serve them cake accompanied by a great cup of coffee or the tea of your choice.

Raise a cake-filled fork to Hillary and the things we do for love.

IF-AT-FIRST LIME CAKE

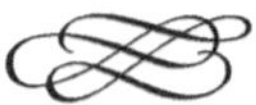

*M*akes 12-16 servings

. . .

I'D QUILTED for seven hours and didn't hate the creations I'd produced, including two Christmas stockings to hang above the fireplace that my house didn't have. My man was visiting his ailing mother out of town, Dakota was on yet another first date (I crossed my fingers, toes, and eyes for her), and everyone else I called had plans that Saturday night or told me they did because they sensed my desperation, or maybe they just didn't like me. That's a bigger club than I like to admit. However, I can live with not being liked by many so long as I'm loved by a few, and I am, so I didn't bog down in complete despair that Saturday night.

But I was more anxiety-riddled than normal. That morning while I was in the office at *Paducah Pulse*, someone threw a brick through the large plate-glass window in the press room. The shattering glass startled me, and the alarm blared before I could reach the press room. I carefully maneuvered my way through the spray of glass until I reached the brick. It was fifty-percent larger than modern-day bricks. The parts of my house that were still upright were supported by similar bricks, each with the word Egyptian embedded in them. I had seen the word in the bricks in my house but never looked up where they came from—until one shattered the window that morning.

I didn't touch the brick, called the police, then swept up the glass. After the officers had investigated, and after a handyman had temporarily filled the gap with plywood, I looked up Egyptian bricks.

Produced by the Murphysboro Paving Brick Company in Murphysboro, Illinois, beginning in 1908, the large bricks became so popular that the United States Government ordered two million bricks for the construction of the Panama Canal. Many streets in Southern Illinois are either still made of exposed bricks, or the bricks have been covered by blacktop.

The distance between Murphysboro and Paducah is about seventy-five miles. Considering the fact that Egyptian bricks made it as far as the Panama Canal, I wasn't surprised that the builders of my house included the extra-hard, durable bricks.

What do bricks have to do with lime cake? Very little, except that they may play a role in my next adventure, and my anxiety that night was caused in part by that flying brick's sudden arrival. I'd thought my enemies had ended their feuds with me, were serving prison time, or had found someone else to harass.

However, my assessment of my enemies was inaccurate, and that had me nervously (okay, obsessively) quilting, then still needing to burn off energy (does anxiety melt, dissipate, or evaporate?).

Therefore, I decided to bake. I looked at the ingredients I had on my counters, in my cupboards, and in my fridge. I decided to make a lime cake. Of course, I could have looked up a recipe for lemon cake, then swapped the juice and zest of one citrus for another. But that seemed too easy. In other words, it didn't sound like me. I occasionally choose to use chopsticks because they're more difficult to use than a fork, at least to most of us raised in the United States.

I knew which ingredients bakers usually use to bake a cake, and I was pretty sure I could ballpark the proportions. The resulting cake would have been very good, if I'd named it The Deconstructed Lime Cake.

I had used non-stick spray instead of buttering-and-flouring the bundt pan, and a third of the cake proved to be more stubborn than a mule on tranquilizers. The cake stuck to the pan while seeming to mock me. I swear I saw a sneer in the remaining hunk of cake.

I gave The Deconstructed Lime cake to Trevor, the boy who lives next door, and his family, saying, "If you eat this cake with your eyes closed, it's very good. I'm going home to make a better, prettier one. If I succeed, I'll give you that one, too, after I sample it, of course."

I increased the amount of lime juice and zest, removed my second attempt from the pan without mishap, drizzled the frosting over what I had now named If-at-First Lime Cake, then brought about half of the cake to Trevor, his two older brothers, and his parents on Sunday morning.

I should have taken the whole cake with me to PQQ that afternoon, but I'd seen the look on Trevor's face when I'd offered him the first cake, and I'd heard the nasty tone in his father's voice and his choice of words when he addressed Trevor and his older brothers, Adam and Joseph, so I brought them the improved cake and said, "I hope you boys enjoy this as much as I did." I couldn't very well tell Ester and Ethan Springfield that they weren't allowed to indulge in any cake, but I wanted to.

Just as I wanted to find out who had thrown the brick.

But, to paraphrase the Rolling Stones, "We can't always get what we want."

Unless we want cake, and then we can bake this one.

PREHEAT **the oven to 350**

    3 cups all-purpose flour
    1 tsp baking powder
    1 tsp baking soda
    2 sticks (1 cup) butter, softened
    1 3/4 cups sugar
    5 eggs
    1/2 cup plus one tablespoon lime juice
    zest of 4 limes
    2 tsps vanilla
    1 cup low-fat buttermilk
    3/4 cup powdered sugar
    1/8 cup heavy cream

WHISK THE FLOUR, baking powder, and baking soda together in a small bowl.

In a large bowl, beat the butter and sugar on high for two minutes.

Add 1/2 cup of lime juice, reserving 1 TBL for the topping

Add zest and vanilla, then mix.

Beat in half the flour mixture on low, then the buttermilk, then the remaining flour mixture.

Butter-and-flour the heck out of your 12-cup bundt pan (or use non-stick spray at your own peril).

Pour batter into pan, then tap pan three-hundred-twelve times on the counter to remove the air bubbles. Or you could do it three or four times, if you're not batty.

Bake at 350 for 50 minutes

Check doneness with a toothpick. Both my cakes were perfectly baked at 53 minutes.

Only let the cake sit in the pan for 10 minutes, then use a knife to free the edges. Remove the cake by inverting the pan. I really hope you didn't need me to tell you that. Coax it out with finesse or whichever kitchen dance you find works best. But not the Lambada, because, as everyone should know by now, that's the forbidden dance.

After the cake has cooled, beat the powdered sugar, the remaining tablespoon of lime juice, and the heavy cream in a bowl, then drizzle the topping over the cake in whichever manner pleases you.

Share the cake with friends, family, neighbors, and passersby, so long as they're not passing by on motorcycles at high speed. That could get messy.

IRISH SODA BREAD

Yeah, right!

Why not just sprinkle sadness on a piece of cardboard?

If you did, you'd get all of the fiber, none of the hassle, and exactly the same amount of deliciousness—none.

MAGNIFICENT MOCHA PANNA COTTA

$\mathcal{M}$akes 5 servings

. . .

I DIDN'T HEAR the word ramekin until I was watching *Chopped* on television, well into adulthood. I didn't hear the words panna cotta until much later when I attended a fancy dinner in Nashville, and the dessert that had just been presented to me wasn't called custard, as I'd expected it would be, but panna cotta. I looked it up and learned that it's Italian for "cooked cream."

I've worked hard to make up for the lack of class, grace, couth, manners, and refinement dispensed by Ellen Carroll to her two daughters, and I believe I've made significant progress in that regard. Some might say I "put on airs" or act "too big for my britches" by not embracing the ungrammatical world that surrounded me, the one in which people clung to convention and the known rather than aspiring to improve themselves and discover the world outside of their home counties. If people think I'm a snob because I prefer grilled salmon to a boiled hot dog, I can live with that—and I'll likely outlive those who do such deeming.

I rarely settle for "good enough." If something is good, perhaps it can be improved until it's great. That's what aspiration and invention are—acknowledgments that the status quo is inadequate. If aspiration wasn't inherent in human beings, I'd be writing this with a quill, or maybe I'd communicate only through grunts and pointing.

In other words, I tasted the vanilla panna cotta in Nashville long ago and thought, "This is absolutely delicious, maybe even perfect."

But as the years went by and I become more comfortable in the kitchen—and after the Paducah Quilters Quorum members all but demanded that I write a cookbook—my confidence grew, and I decided to look up a recipe for panna cotta. Of course, I found many dozens online, and the recipe I chose proved to be every bit as delicious as the panna cotta I'd eaten in Nashville.

But then I did what I do: I asked, "What if …"

"What if in addition to vanilla I infused the recipe with espresso powder?" I was certain many versions of espresso panna cotta must exist, so I didn't bother to look them up. Instead, I decided to add both espresso powder and cocoa to a basic panna cotta recipe, modifying the original by upping the sugar content to offset the bitterness imparted by the espresso and cocoa. Then I metaphorically crossed my fingers as I placed the ramekins in the refrigerator to set overnight.

Panna cotta traditionally isn't a breakfast food, but, heck, my version has cream, espresso, sugar, and chocolate, so it's practically a specialty drink from Starbucks.

In other words, in the name of science, I devoured a mocha panna cotta the next morning. In order for me to name it accurately, I had to be sure of the first one's magnificence by downing a second—after all, the scientific method requires replicability. Thankfully, the second was identical to the first, enabling me accurately to impart the name Magnificent Mocha Panna Cotta to the dessert—or breakfast—I'd created.

1 PINT HEAVY cream
    1/2 cup sugar
    1 tsp vanilla extract
    1 tsp vanilla paste (if you can't find it, double the extract)
    1 tsp cocoa powder
    1 tsp espresso powder
    1 1/8 tsps unflavored gelatin
    1 1/2 TBLs milk

FINDING espresso powder can be a challenge. I ordered mine online. You may be tempted to skip this step, but you also may be tempted to skip out on paying your taxes, skip town, and skip to my Lou, and I don't want any part of any of those. But let's face it: Some of you—I won't name names—are going to do what you want, so if your panna cotta turns out less-than-stellar, don't blame me.

Pour the heavy cream into a saucepan. Medium is probably best, but you may have a favorite saucepan, or even a lucky one, so use whichever saucepan makes you feel at ease (by the way, although this dessert tastes as decadent as any you've eaten, and guests will likely be impressed by your culinary skill in rendering such an extravagant dessert, you will be surprised by how easy it is to create these. The difficult part is letting them set up. Trust me: I've had to slap a hand or two trying to pilfer one before they're set—and one of those hands was mine).

Turn the burner to medium and be prepared to pay attention. If you get distracted by your kids, the dog, your husband showing you a "weird thing" on his back, or an incoming asteroid, your dessert will be ruined. That scalded outcome should be unacceptable in all of the above examples except the asteroid strike. If it's a near miss, then it would be a shame to have wasted the ingredients. If it's a strike, well, I'm pretty sure Magnificent Mocha Panna Cotta is on the menu in Heaven.

Add the sugar, vanilla extract, and vanilla paste.

Stir until it all dissolves and incorporates.

Stir in the cocoa powder, doing your best to eliminate any chunks.

Stir in the espresso powder until the liquid has a consistency in the neighborhood of homogeneity. Don't panic. I'm not promoting any particular lifestyle. Unless eating well can be considered a lifestyle. If so, then I'm guilty as charged.

Dance for twelve seconds. You can't risk the mixture going beyond a simmer. Okay, you probably could have danced for a whole song, provided it wasn't "American Pie" or Beethoven's Symphony No. 9. If your happy feet are able to do their thing while you watch the pot, then dance away. The adage about a watched pot is untrue, by the way, as anyone who's ruined a panna cotta can attest.

When bubbles appear around the edges, stir one last time, putting a flourish that only you know how to do into the gesture, even though no one is likely watching, then remove the pot from the heat, put the lid on, and set a timer for fifteen minutes.

This really is the best time for a true dance break. If you can't find a partition, use a woven chair (copyright issues).

After you've boogied yourself silly, sprinkle the gelatin over the milk in a small bowl. It doesn't matter to me which color bowl you use, although it may matter to you. If so, you may be taking this recipe too seriously—so do another dance move now, then let the recipe work its magic, regardless of the bowl color.

Stir the gelatin so that it semi-sorta dissolves. Let it sit for five minutes.

When the allotted fifteen minutes have passed (meaning the timer has gone off), put the pot back on the burner, then bring the contents to a simmer. When the simmer is simmering, remove the pot from the heat and add the gelatin/milk mixture.

Stir the pot. I mean that literally. If you like to do so figuratively—for example, bringing up Uncle Will's drinking problem at the Thanksgiving table while he's sitting at it—well, please invite me to your house next November. You obviously know how to bring things to a boil, so to speak.

But please tell me you haven't gotten distracted and let the liquid you've been tending to boil. I understand that life can be chaotic and our attention is pulled in all directions. But pay attention, and exercise patience and restraint.

You may be tempted to call what you've just created a hot toddy, then down it once it's cool enough. Don't do it. Sure, your Uncle Will would upend his flask into the chocolatey elixir, then run off with the pot so he could down it all himself. But you're better than that.

Pour the liquid into five ramekins, or into coffee cups, or martini glasses, or your son's sneakers (just checking whether you stopped reading to down the delicious elixir because you are not, in fact, better than your Uncle Will).

Let the liquid deliciousness cool, then cover each ramekin, coffee cup, martini glass, or sneaker with cling wrap.

Set whichever vessels you've chosen in the refrigerator. Set up a perimeter (crime-scene tape works well, but so do fabric bolts lying horizontally between chairs—either wooden or woven).

This line of defense is necessary because anyone who knows you are making this dessert will find an excuse to stop watching reruns of *Murder, She Wrote* to slip into the kitchen to see if the panna cotta are firm yet. The way they will do this is by eating one. Do not allow this to happen.

You worked hardly at all over the course of very little time to prepare this dessert, so you are darn tootin' not going to let just anyone waltz into your kitchen to enjoy something now that you will gladly allow them to enjoy later.

Now that I've written that, maybe semi-set panna cotta is also delicious. I'd wait at least three and a half hours—or overnight—but do whatever feels right.

MEMPHIS MELODIES — PECAN PIE REIMAGINED

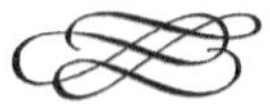

*M*akes 12 large squares

. . .

DURING ONE OF my almost weekly pilgrimages to Ventura, California, from UCLA, Bruce asked me if I wanted to sample a baked good that his mother, Barbara, had invented the night before and had named Memphis Melodies, in keeping with the blues theme of The Blues Bakery.

"Of course," I said, excited to taste the latest delight from my favorite establishment. But I could tell something was wrong. Bruce's energy was off, and he was wearing a brace on his right wrist.

He removed a pan from the refrigerator, used a spatula to remove a corner piece, then used a bakery tissue to hand the dessert to me.

"Thank you. What happened to your wrist?" I asked before I took a bite.

"Tendonitis. It's in both wrists, and the doctor refused to believe I'm right handed, based on how much function I've lost. More than seventy-five percent, he estimated. I couldn't hold a fork to make an egg wash this morning. I had to use my left hand. I was hoping carpal tunnel caused the pain because the surgery for that is relatively simple. But the only cure for tendonitis is to stop using the tendons. Too many repetitive motions, plus I must have weak tendons. What I hoped would be my budding high school basketball career ended when I got tendonitis in my right foot. The situation is tough, but life goes on."

"I'm so sorry." I knew it would be rude to bite into the Memphis Melody while he was telling me about his injuries, so I waited and asked, "Please don't tell me what you're about to tell me."

He nodded toward the dessert and said, "Go ahead. Don't let the bad news influence your assessment of my mom's latest creation. It's kind of a reimagined pecan pie that uses a modified version of our lemon bar crust."

I took a bite, and the crunch of the pecans, the sweetness of the filling, and the richness of the crust improved my worldview. I no longer felt that humanity was doomed. To my knowledge, a baked good had never ended a war, but had anyone at least *tried* to bring both sides to the bargaining table by providing a confection that nearly everyone could agree was excellent? If warring factions could agree that human palates are far more similar than different, then perhaps finding common ground on nuclear disarmament isn't too far behind. If The Blues Bakery's Best-Ever Peanut Butter Cookies and Memphis Melodies were served on the negotiating table, even sworn enemies would at least belly up to it.

But, between bites as I was amusing myself with these thoughts, I couldn't help feeling sad because I realized what Bruce was telling me. I looked at the white logo painted on the brick wall, surrounded by posters of blues concerts and various musical memorabilia. The electric guitar on the wall had been given to Bruce by Pat Benatar and her husband, guitarist, and musical collaborator, Neil Giraldo. Their blues CD, *True Love*, played in The Blues Bakery as I asked, "This is extraordinary. Please let your mother know how great they are. Are you saying you have to close?"

"Not close but sell. Our largest account, The Daily Grind, lost its lease, and the owner of a different shop who verbally committed to purchasing twice as much as The Daily Grind backed out without even telling me. I showed up with the first day's order, as we'd agreed upon, and she looked at me like I was trying to steal from her. Obviously, I needed a contract, but I didn't have one with any of the other accounts, so I didn't think I needed one with her. Silly me: I trusted her."

"I'm sorry. That's awful. When it sells, what are you going to do?"

"I don't think I told you this, but the plan when my mom and I opened this place was for me to run it well enough so that I could hire a manager, step away, then write mysteries. It didn't work out as planned."

"Maybe it will one day."

PREHEAT OVEN to 300

FOR THE CRUST:
   3/4 cup (1 1/2 sticks) butter, melted

1/2 cup powdered sugar
1 1/4 cups flour
1/4 cup cocoa powder

MIX the still-hot butter with the powdered sugar, flour, and cocoa powder until a ball forms.

Place the ball in the center of the pan, then use the heel of your hand and your fingers to spread the dough throughout the pan until it is very thin and reaches about three-quarters of an inch up the sides. The phrase "Patience is a virtue" applies here, and if you're a quilter whose meticulously constructed a Four Winds quilt block, you have all the patience you need.

BAKE at 300 for 20 minutes

FOR THE FILLING:
3 eggs, beaten
2 cups pecans, chopped
1 cup light corn syrup
2 TBLs butter, melted
1 1/2 tsps vanilla

MIX all of the filling ingredients thoroughly.

Pour into the crust, spreading the filling into the corners and evening it.

Bake at 300 for 37 minutes

Let cool to room temperature, then set the pan in the refrigerator for at least three hours, preferably overnight.

"Again with the patience," you're probably saying. "Why can't she just create a recipe I can eat when I'm done? It's like she's gotta do everything the hard way. She probably makes her own soap."

No, I don't make my own soap, smart aleck, but now that you've put that possibility in my head …

Bruce showed me how to create twelve large bars by setting the pan perpendicular to me, then carefully slicing down the middle of the pan. I cut each of those halves in half, then I rotate the pan and cut the length of the pan twice, more or less equally, creating twelve bars. Most people would probably deem the resulting twelve bars to be too large for consumption by an individual.

However, because the bars that The Blues Bakery served were that size, I honor the bakery's memory by continuing the tradition begun in the late 1990s by Bruce and his mom, Barbara.

MATT'S OATMEAL RAISIN
COOKIES

Makes 18 to 20 large cookies

. . .

I'LL ADMIT this publicly for the first time: I really dislike—okay, can't stand—coconut, unless I scoop it out of its shell. In other words, you won't find a recipe for macaroons in this cookbook.

Of course, that statement would be unnecessary if Matt, my ex-fiancé, hadn't included sweetened coconut flakes in his oatmeal raisin cookies—his secret ingredient. I reminded him twice that he also included a proprietary spice mix that contained other secret ingredients. He either pretended not to hear me both times, or he acknowledged by his silence that I'd won the argument.

It's considered bad manners to speak ill of the dead—which is especially true of those who have been murdered—so I will heed conventions of politeness by not denigrating Matt. I will, however, say that he was as uncomfortable in the kitchen as I would be in a lion's den. This is not a knock against him—only a statement of fact. He spent only a little more time preparing meals, eating, and cleaning up than I spend scouring my backyard with a metal detector looking for buried Civil War loot—and I don't own a metal detector.

But Matt could prepare one item in the kitchen that I not only would eat but would also look forward to eating: oatmeal raisin cookies.

During one of the rare moments when he revealed vulnerable parts of himself to me, he told me that when he first arrived in Paducah, after fleeing Philadelphia with his mother, Donna, she taught him how to make the following recipe. He was ten years old, and she walked him through every step, introducing him to the implements needed and explaining which functions each served. Then she guided him through the preparation and baking.

He told me he never felt as good about himself as he did when he completed that task, then ate one scrumptious cookie after another. I find it sad that a man who accomplished as much as he did couldn't find something more significant to take pride in, but he never put his troubled childhood behind him, and trauma stays with many of us forever. So, he found self-esteem where he could—in the shared experience of baking oatmeal raisin cookies with his mother.

Despite all of the positive developments that have shaped my life since he died, I still think of him often. Every time I bake his cookies, I think of the laughs we shared. Then I raise a cookie in his honor and say, "Thank you, Mattie. I hope you're at peace."

I never eat that cookie. I always give that one away.

I give most of the others away, too, but I keep track of which one is Matt's, and I usually give that one to the sad little boy who lives next-door named Trevor. The smile he flashes after taking the first bite reminds me of the smile on Matt's face when he'd nail a guitar lick he'd been struggling to master. I tell myself that the smile on Trevor's face is similar to the one on Matt's the first time he tasted the cookies that he and his mom baked together.

PREHEAT OVEN **to 350**

   1 stick butter (1/4 pound), softened

   3/8 cup sugar

   3/8 cup brown sugar

   1/2 tsp vanilla

   1/3 cup sweetened coconut flakes

   2 eggs

   1 tsp baking soda

   1 1/2 cups flour

   2 1/2 cups oatmeal

   3/4 cups raisins

   1 cup chopped walnuts (optional. But then, so is everything else in this recipe. Instead of baking another batch of cookies, you could be curing cancer or—*gasp!*—organizing your fabric stash)

   1 tsp spice mix (1/2 TBL cinnamon; 3/4 tsp nutmeg; 1/2 tsp allspice; zest of one lemon or one orange)

IN A VERY LARGE mixing bowl (or, ideally, in the bowl of a stand mixer), cream the butter, sugar, brown sugar, vanilla, spice mix, and shredded coconut.

Add eggs, then mix.

Add baking soda and flour, then mix.

Add oatmeal, then mix.

Add raisins and walnuts, then mix.

Scoop onto baking sheets (or silicone baking mats within the baking sheets) in balls roughly the size of a golf ball.

Use a hand-sized piece of wax paper or parchment paper to press down on the cookies with your palm—enough to turn them into thickish discs, not pancakes.

Bake at 350 for 12 minutes

Of course, you don't have to raise a cookie to honor Matt, but you may want to honor loved ones you've lost by preparing their favorite meals every so often. It works for me.

MRS. CROWLEY'S SUGAR COOKIES

he number of servings depends on the size of your
cookie cutters

. . .

WHEN I WAS TEN, I was riding a borrowed bike around town when I ran over a nail on Jefferson, and the tire went flat. I didn't have tire tools, a patch kit, or a spare inner tube, and I didn't know how to repair a flat, even if I'd been carrying any of those biking essentials.

I had a long walk home to our Elmwood Court apartment. I was walking on the sidewalk along South 28th, feeling awful because I didn't have money to fix Michelle's tire, and my mom would not only refuse to help me pay for it but would, if I was lucky, only berate me for causing the tire to go flat, instead of beating me.

I happened to look up as a silver mini-van approached with the most gorgeous girl I'd ever seen looking at me through the open window—red hair flowing past her shoulders and delicate features that made me wonder if doll manufacturers used her face as a model. Her expression went from neutral to concerned as the van passed. I turned to watch it drive away, and it took an abrupt right, as if the driver hadn't planned soon enough to make the turn.

I kept walking. A minute later, the van pulled to the curb near the intersection I was approaching. The beautiful girl got out and jogged toward me.

"Hi, I'm Dakota," she said. "Dakota Crowley."

"Hi, I'm Hadley Carroll."

She was older and significantly taller than I was and had the curves I hoped some day to have. I'd never even dreamed of owning the designer clothes she wore. My shorts, t-shirt, and sneakers had been old when I'd chosen them at the Salvation Army, and they were all a size too small.

Dakota wore a black Calvin Klein tracksuit, spotless white Reebok running shoes, and a watch that looked more expensive than my mom's ancient Ford Pinto, which meant the watch had to cost at least $400. She wore a pin near the top of the track suit that I leaned in to read. It said, National Quilt Museum.

"I like your pin," I said. "Are you a quilter?"

"Yes," she said. She smiled, and the warmth and acceptance emanating from her radiant face changed the trajectory of my life. I wanted more of whatever she was offering.

"So am I. Well, I've quilted, but I'm not really a quilter."

"If you're up for it, I can help you become a quilter. Let's take care of your bike. Then, if your parents are okay with it, I'll show you some techniques at our house that will make you a quilter. We have a pretty good stash room."

I didn't tell her the bike wasn't mine, or that I didn't know my father, or that my mom wouldn't care where I was, or that my tattered thrift-store clothes embarrassed me, or that I'd only quilted a few times with my mom and sister and had never heard of a stash room. What I said instead was, "That's really nice of you, but I should probably take care of the bike myself. I'm the one who got the flat."

"Don't be silly, Hadley. We'll get it fixed in no time, then if your parents—"

"My mom won't care if I go to your house, and my sister's playing at a neighbor's."

She introduced me to her mother, Ann, and her younger sister, Cathy, then scooted the bike between the seats. Ann told us she'd leave us at their house, then take care of the bike.

When we drove down the driveway toward their house, I tried not to let my jaw drop. The door to the four-car garage was open, and just the shine on the three cars made me realize I was about to experience a world far different than my daily reality. I learned later that the cars were a Jaguar sedan, a Porsche 911, and a classic Mercedes 280 SLC.

The house was as stunning as the cars and as well-maintained. I wanted to shout how amazing all of it was, but I'm glad I didn't because after Dakota, Cathy, and I had been quilting for two hours, Dakota said to me, "I liked you right away. Do you want to know why?"

"Yes."

"Because you didn't tell me how pretty I am. I understand that many people think I'm attractive, but when I look in the mirror, I find something new I don't like about myself almost daily. Being told I'm gorgeous and our house is amazing and our cars are classics has nothing to do with me. I didn't accomplish any of those. I've never received a grade lower than an A, and I'm going to be a lawyer, but no one except my parents and teachers ever acknowledge what I've actually accomplished. You pointed out the pin, not my clothes. I chose my outfit, but I didn't buy it. But I chose the pin and bought it, and it's important because quilting and the National Quilt Museum are important to me."

I'd wanted to tell her that her beauty had rendered me speechless and that the Crowley home filled me with admiration and envy, so I'm glad I didn't. Had I gone gaga over her and the house, who knows if we would have become best friends and if I would have become a quilter?

When Mrs. Crowley returned from BikeWorld, where she got the tire fixed, she asked us if we'd like to take a break from quilting to help her bake cookies.

"Yes, ma'am," I said as Dakota said, "You know I'm not comfortable in the kitchen, Momma," and Cathy said, "I guess."

Mrs. Crowley proved to be the kindest, friendliest person I'd ever met, and as she walked me through the steps she used to make the cookie dough, I wondered for the thousandth time what had happened to my mom to make her so different than Mrs. Crowley.

Dakota chose the heart-shaped cookie cutters, and we three girls cut out the cookies after Mrs. Crowley showed me how to roll out the dough.

PREHEAT OVEN to 350

1/4 POUND BUTTER, **softened**
   1/2 cup plus 1 TBL sugar
   1 1/2 tsps vanilla
   1 egg
   1 TBL milk
   1 1/2 cups flour
   3/4 tsp baking powder

. . .

Cream together the butter, sugar, and vanilla, then add the egg and mix. Add the milk, then mix.

If you feel persnickety, sift the flour and baking powder together before you add the combination to the wet ingredients. However, if you regularly throw caution to the wind and have left your fabric scissors where someone could use them to cut paper, cardboard, or baling wire, then feel free to pour the flour and the baking powder directly into the wet ingredients. Either way, you'll survive, unlike your fabric scissors or anyone who uses them for a purpose other than the one for which they were designed.

When the dough comes together, form it into a ball, then chill the bowl in the refrigerator. After the dough has chilled, flour a large surface (preferably a cutting board or counter, not your square quilting ruler) and a rolling pin, then roll the dough out until it's approximately a quarter inch thick.

Work quickly because the dough becomes soft and unmanageable if you're not handy with a rolling pin, to paraphrase the musical and movie *Oliver*.

Use whichever cookie cutters suit your mood to cut out the cookies. Set them on a cookie sheet, then gather the left-over dough and repeat the process.

Bake at 350 for ten to twelve minutes

If you feel compelled to frost them, be my guest. If you prefer to douse them in powdered sugar, I won't judge you. If you eat all of the cookies in one sitting, you should wipe the crumbs from your lips, then call an ambulance.

After we'd eaten our fill of cookies and settled back in to quilt, I felt guilty about having kept so much of who I was and what I'd felt about Dakota and her home from her that I told her that I'd borrowed the bike from Michelle.

Mrs. Crowley drove me home, and I returned Michelle's bike to her.

The next afternoon, Dakota knocked on our apartment door. I smiled and said hello, but I noticed an expression I didn't recognize when she said, "Hi, Hadley."

"What's wrong?" I asked.

"Nothing, really, but I'm not sure this is the right thing to do, but all I can do is try. I've grown nearly six inches in the last three years, so Daddy recently bought me a new bike. My old one's perfectly fine. I outgrew it, so it's just been sitting in the garage. If you're okay with me doing so, I'd like to give it to you."

"If you're not playing a joke, of course, that would be fantastic. I can't believe you'd do that for me. We just met."

"No joke, and even though we just met, I think we 'hit it off,' as Daddy says, don't you?"

"Definitely."

"Well, if you'd like the bike, it's in the van just around the corner."

"Thank you so much. Maybe we can ride together."

"That's what I'm hoping."

The Sage Green Unisex Peugeot was in near-perfect shape, fit me well, and gave me four years of joy, until I outgrew the bike.

Dakota and I didn't really become cyclists—as opposed to casual bike riders—until decades later, but we rode together plenty around town, often before or after quilting together.

In other words, I will forever be grateful to that fateful nail.

NOTHING-LIKE-CARDBOARD
BRAN MUFFINS

*M*akes 16 muffins

. . .

No, I'm not calling you old.

You don't have to eat bran muffins, nor am I suggesting you do. I'm merely here presenting words and pictures for your perusal. Should you choose to make this recipe, your reasons are your own, unless you're on Facebook, in which case your reasons will likely be commented upon by the world.

Facebook isn't your therapist, folks. It's a way to stay in touch with people you didn't feel the need to keep in touch with before Facebook existed, but suddenly where Gillian from second grade ate lunch today is really important!

In other words, would I post a picture on Facebook of the hardwood floor that has been scuffed, scarred, and Trapunto'd to the extent that I don't walk around barefoot for fear that a toothpick-sized splinter will lodge itself in my flesh? No, I will not.

Not again.

I made the mistake of sharing a picture of a painting I'd painted, but the state of the floor under the painting was the only element of the photo that anyone cared do comment on, and by comment I mean criticized as though I'd damaged *their* floors, then charged them for my handiwork.

In other words, I won't foist photos of my home onto Facebook, and I'll fix my floors when I get to them. Whether you choose to eat bran muffins is your call.

Anyway, I used to think bran muffins were a form of torture, a version of washing our mouths out with soap.

But soap tasted better.

So, why, you ask, have I included a recipe for bran muffins? Because one morning Bruce had sold out of every other muffin at The Blues Bakery, which to me confirmed my assessment of the coarse cardboard-tasting items. When I noticed that he had two left, I asked, "How many bran muffins did you bake today?"

"A dozen."

"Meaning ten people bought the others?"

"You sound skeptical." He smiled. "What else would I have done with them? Mopped up an oil spill? Insulated the walls with them?"

I laughed.

"Sorry, I said. "I didn't mean to insult you."

"You haven't insulted me. But you have shown contempt prior to investigation, which isn't a sound policy for anyone, let alone someone who wants to be a reporter."

"I *am* a reporter. I write for the *Daily Bruin* and a local paper."

"Than report on this." He reached into the display case with a bakery tissue, removed a muffin that was bigger than his fist, and handed it to me.

"Thank you," I said. "I eat my muffins with butter. Do you have any?"

"This is a bakery, so, yes, I have plenty of butter. Take a bite, without butter, as though you've never had a bran muffin before, assess it honestly, then let me know if you need butter."

I took a bite, chewed, swallowed, made a happy face, took another bite, chewed, swallowed and said, "I was wrong. Not only does it not need butter, but I also have apparently never had a bran muffin before."

"No more contempt prior to investigation?"

"Not with baked goods, anyway."

"That's a start."

PREHEAT OVEN to 350
   3 cups wheat bran
   1 cup brown sugar
   2/3 cup water, HOT
   2/3 cup honey
   2 eggs, beaten
   2 cups low-fat buttermilk
   2/3 tsp vanilla
   1/2 cup canola oil
   2/3 tsp salt
   1 1/3 tsps cinnamon
   1 1/3 TBLs baking soda

2 2/3 cups flour
1 cup raisins

In a large mixing bowl, combine the bran and brown sugar, then add the hot water and mix.

Add the honey, eggs, buttermilk, vanilla, and canola oil, then mix.

Add the salt, cinnamon, baking soda, and flour.

Mix until incorporated, then add the raisins.

Using two baking tins with a dozen cups each, grease and flour, spray with non-stick spray, or use baking cups—or some combination thereof—sixteen cups.

Of course, if you only have one tin, and you're mathematically inclined, you could cut the above recipe down by one quarter (12 is three-quarters of 16), but because I don't know how to add half an egg to a recipe, I'd rather make more muffins or bake two batches than perform surgery on an egg yolk.

Fill each cup to the brim, then **bake at 350 for 24 minutes**.

As I've stated elsewhere (but I can't be sure you're reading each recipe in the order I've presented them, so I'll risk redundancy while being informative), your oven may differ from mine. I hope so—mine bakes unevenly, as though one side isn't even trying. Our baking times, therefor, may vary.

Insert a toothpick in a muffin. If it comes out dry, the muffins are finished (or overbaked, so you may want to check at the 22-minute mark). If wet, give them a little more time.

NOT-TOO-SWEET-POTATO PIE

*M*akes one 9-inch pie

. . .

I MET Denise Robinson in calculus class at Paducah Tilghman High School. She earned a perfect score on every test. I made an A in that class but struggled to do so. I wasn't surprised when Denise received a scholarship to Stanford University. Although we've lost touch—meaning she's not on Facebook—I hope she's happy

One Friday afternoon we were talking after class when she asked, "If you don't have anything else going on, would you like to join my family and me tomorrow at a dog show? My dad raises German Shepards. It probably sounds boring, but it's kind of fun."

She had never asked me to do anything outside of school, so I wasn't sure what prompted her to initiate a friendship off campus. I caught myself before I spun into a dark vortex filled with possible motivations. Instead of giving in to my anxiety and insecurity, I said, "That sounds great. Should I bring anything?"

"No. Well, maybe a sweater. If my dad's dogs do well, the event can run into the afternoon, and a breeze could kick up."

"Great. I'm looking forward to it."

"We'll be there at 9. You're in the Elmwood Court, right?"

I didn't want to say yes because that sprawl of apartments wasn't among the nicer addresses in Paducah. It was not a palace, and I had nothing but other dumpy apartments to compare it to. If she'd given me a choice, I would've told her to pick me up at Red's Donuts, not far from our sorry apartment. But because somehow she knew where I lived, I said, "Yes. See you at 9. And thank you for inviting me."

I enjoyed most of the dog show (it became tiresome after the third hour), but I enjoyed every aspect of hanging out with Denise, her two younger sisters, Flo and Carla, and her parents, Eunice and Horace.

They got along so well and loved each other so much that I started to think they were putting on a "happy family" act for my benefit because my mother, sister, and I had never spent three hours together without criticisms, anger, and resentment flaring up. But when I joined the Robinsons for dinner at their impressive home in West Paducah, I realized I was in the presence of the third truly happy family I'd met, the first two being the Crowleys and the Veneziales.

After we ate a delicious turkey casserole accompanied by cornbread, Mrs. Robinson asked if I'd like a slice of sweet potato pie.

"I've never had it, but, yes, please."

"Never tasted sweet potato pie? Well, you didn't grow up in my house, that's for sure. Holidays would see four or five bakers competing for bragging rights. The winner was the one whose pie disappeared first."

"Then the arguments started," Mr. Robinson said, and we laughed.

"Mama's is best," Denise said, "even if she didn't win every year."

"Won more than my share. But I don't want to put pressure on you. If you don't like it, Hadley, I won't be offended."

I nodded and took a bite. The texture, spice mix, and amount of sugar were perfect. However, I thought the crust was a little dry.

"It's amazing, Mrs. Robinson. Excellent."

When I took my second bite, including a dollop of the homemade whipped cream on top, I thought, "This is *almost* a perfect bite of pie."

Denise and I became close the rest of the year, before we both headed to college in California. Mrs. Robinson, as a going-away present, gave me the recipe on the day I said goodbye to them.

The recipe for the filling below replicates Mrs. Robinson's exactly. The crust, however, is all mine, the same shortbread crust I use for my lemon bars. If you prefer a traditional crust or have one that's been passed down from previous generations of your family, please feel free to use it. Neither Mrs. Robinson nor I will be upset.

But if you don't, at least one time, make a sweet-potato pie from scratch (okay, fine, use a store-bought crust, but your guests will talk about you on their way home), Mrs. Robinson and I may be less forgiving. The offense won't kill us, certainly, but we may be a touch standoffish when we run into you in Kroger.

PREHEAT OVEN to 300

For the crust:

1/2 pound butter, melted

2 1/2 cups flour

1/2 cup plus 1 1/2 TBLs powdered sugar

MIX the still-hot butter with the 2 1/2 cups of flour and the powdered sugar until a ball forms.

Place the ball in the center of the 9-inch pie pan, then use the heel of your hand and your fingers to spread the dough throughout the pan until it is very thin on the bottom and spreads evenly up the sides, with enough thickness left over to form a decent crust around the rim.

If you want to try to roll out your traditional crust instead, that's fine. One of the reasons I developed this crust is because I'm not good with a rolling pin. My pizzas look like Picasso paintings, and my pie crusts would be perfect if pans were shaped like rhomboids.

Again, if you feel more comfortable using your go-to pie crust recipe, more power to you. Of course, you should use whichever technique you prefer to crimp the top. I use a fork because, well, I don't care all that much about presentation.

Unless we're talking quilts.

Bake at 300 for 20 minutes

then

Reset oven to 350

FOR THE FILLING:

2 large sweet potatoes, peeled and softened via microwave or by boiling

3 eggs

1/2 cup milk

1/4 cup heavy cream

2/3 cup sugar

1 tsp vanilla

1/8 tsp salt

1 tsp cinnamon

1/4 tsp cloves

1/2 tsp allspice
1/2 tsp nutmeg
1/2 tsp ginger

IF YOU PREFER to use somewhere in the neighborhood of 2 teaspoons of pumpkin pie spice mix, I won't tell anyone, but you'll know, and if you have trouble sleeping that night, who are you going to blame? Me? Well, good luck with that because I listed the ingredients necessary, yet you chose to take a short cut. Look, if you insist on willy-nillying your way through the recipes, perhaps we can work out an hourly rate that will satisfy us both so I can bake your pies for you.

But perhaps it would be best for you to follow the recipes as written, then declare me an incompetent buffoon devoid of taste or tastebuds when you deem the recipes suboptimal. But then, you could like them, and that would make me happy, and we can all use more happiness, especially when it comes baked.

Mash the sweet potatoes, then zap them with a hand mixer or blitz them in a Cuisinart—whatever it takes to take them from stringy to smooth.

Add the eggs and mix until incorporated.

Add all of the other ingredients, then blend as though your life depends on it. I'm not saying it does, but I can't guarantee it doesn't. How do I know if someone will burst into your kitchen and demand a perfectly blended pie, or else ...

Pour the filling into the crust.

Bake at 350 for 50 minutes

IF YOU WANT to bake at a scalding temperature for a while, then lower the temp, then bake for a while, then cover the crust with tin foil, you have more patience than I do. I followed the recipe as written, and I was pleased with the result. Okay, more than pleased but not giddy. I don't think I've ever been giddy. Dr. Elaine Bourget has tried to convince me I'm entitled to giddiness, but I haven't quite embraced her assessment. I'm trying, really. Baby steps.

I'll forever be grateful to Denise and her family for introducing me to sweet potato pie and to Mrs. Robinson for giving me the recipe.

As we said our goodbyes, Mrs. Robinson wished me good luck at UCLA, handed me the recipe, and said, "I hope you enjoy this for years to come, Hadley. But remember—never a store-bought crust."

PADUCAH CHEESECAKE

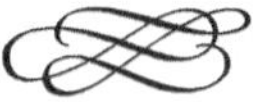

$\mathcal{M}$akes one 8-inch cheesecake, typically shared

. . .

THE FIRST TIME I ate cheesecake was at the tenth birthday party of a classmate named Cynthia (I've forgotten her last name, and if I really cared, I could probably find her on Facebook, but her last name isn't relevant to this anecdote, so I don't care enough to track her down. Actually, neither her first nor her last name is important to this anecdote, which is really just a chronology of my cheesecake-eating progression).

I liked the cheesecake that day. However, two years earlier I'd also liked the birthday cake that included hazelnuts at Cecilia Jenkins' eighth birthday party, and those of you who have read *Quilt City: Panic in Paducah* know how that turned out.

My point is that many people grow up eating Sara Lee Cheesecakes, technically Sara Lee Frozen Bakery Cheesecakes, and many people enjoy them. I'll admit that letting a cake you removed from the freezer thaw, then simply slicing it is easier than making a cheesecake from scratch.

But it's also easier not to wear clothes, yet society and the law deem strolling buck naked through downtown while playing a kazoo to be both unacceptable and illegal.

The kazoo part isn't illegal but probably should be.

Sure, my analogy isn't perfect, but what I'm saying is: Just because something is easy to do doesn't make it worth doing.

After I'd scrimped for two years so I could visit New York City, my world and worldview expanded. Yes, some restaurants in Paducah might have served New York cheesecake when I was growing up, but I never indulged in its cakey wonders until I stepped into a bakery in the theater district and said to the clerk behind the display case, "It's my first time in New York. What would you suggest I try?"

"The cheesecake, darling," said a woman of a certain age who winked as she said it. Coming from her, the wink and her use of "darling" to address a stranger sat well with me. I don't know why, but it was probably because I was in a great mood after having seen *August: Osage County*, the best play I'd seen until then and since.

Referring to the bakery's cheesecake, she said, "It's to die for, and that phrase means something here. We're New York for a reason."

The slice of strawberry cheesecake that day was five inches high and was so dense I had to apply real force to move the fork through it. Delicious is too simple a word to describe the complexity of tastes that combined to make that dessert among the most memorable I've eaten. I went back the next night and tried the blueberry cheesecake, which was also better than delicious.

When I returned home and recovered from the significant financial hit to the extent that I could entertain the idea of eating dessert again, I set out to invent a cheesecake that I could call my own, one that would have elements of New York cheesecake but wouldn't be as dense as the two slices I ate while on that trip.

The following recipe is the one I settled on, although I don't consider it settling.

To many people, cream cheese means Philadelphia Cream Cheese (Matt refused to eat any other kind, saying to me once in the Kroger on Park, "There *isn't* any other kind"). To honor Matt, I use the brand-name cream cheese, but you should use whichever brand your budget can afford.

I considered various names for this recipe but decided on the one above because it sounds right and because I developed it in my kitchen in Lower Town.

If you're feeling lazy and are considering buying a store-bought graham-cracker pie crust instead of making the crust in this recipe, go to your room and rethink your approach to life.

The crust is the crust from the lemon bars. If you follow the recipe as written, not only will you have a scrumptious cheesecake, but you'll also have enough dough left over to make a batch of shortbread cookies, because that's basically what the lemon bar crust is: a shortbread cookie recipe. Of course, you can cut down the recipe to try to save a few pretty pennies, but in this case, more is more. Having extra crust is far better than not having enough. In addition, not everyone likes cheesecake, but nearly everyone but vegans likes shortbread cookies, so I suggest sticking with the recipe as written.

But a graham cracker crust is fine. You caught me in a good mood because I'm recalling how much I enjoyed seeing *August: Osage County* and spending time in New York.

PREHEAT OVEN to 300 degrees
For the crust:
1/2 pound butter, melted
2 1/4 cups flour
1/2 cup plus 1 1/2 TBLs powdered sugar

MIX the still-hot butter with the 2 1/4 cups of flour and the powdered sugar until a ball forms.

Place the ball in the center of the pan, then use the heel of your hand and your fingers to spread the dough throughout the pan until it is very thin and reaches about three-quarters of an inch up the sides. Exude patience as you get the crust just so. Pretend you're quilting, during which you have on many occasions made weeks disappear while you patiently crafted perfection.

BAKE at 300 degrees for 20 minutes
For the filling:
2 8-ounce packages Philadelphia Original Cream Cheese, softened
1/4 cup sugar
2 eggs
1 tsp vanilla
2 TBLs cocoa powder
1 TBL flour
6 ounces of chocolate, melted (whichever kind tickles your taste buds. I used semi-sweet chocolate chips for this recipe. Next time, I'll try dark chocolate but bump up the sugar a little. I'm nothing if not adaptable).

Spray or butter-and-flour an 8-inch spring-form pan.

While the chocolate is melting (preferably in a double-boiler), blend the cream cheese and the sugar until combined.

Add vanilla and eggs one at a time, beating the mixture after each.

Mix in the cocoa powder.

Mix in the melted chocolate.

Pour the batter into the crust in the spring-form pan, then spread the batter to the edges and level it.

Bake at 350 for between 65 and 75 minutes, depending on when the toothpick you insert into the middle comes out dry.

Do not share this recipe with friends and family. You paid for this book, so you are rightfully entitled to keep its contents secret. You don't even have to share the cheesecake with them, come to think of it. But if you feel inclined to let others know that they, too, can withhold the recipe from *their* friends and family simply by buying this book, well, who am I to stop you from doing what you feel inclined to do?

PRIZED PUMPKIN MUFFINS

*M*akes 9 muffins

. . .

PREHEAT OVEN to 350

¾ **stick butter, melted and cooled**

2 eggs

¾ **cup sugar**

¼ **tsp vanilla**

5 ounces pumpkin puree

¼ **cup low-fat buttermilk**

1 ½ tsps cinnamon

A scant ½ tsp cloves

A scant ¼ tsp salt

¾ **TBL baking powder**

1 ½ cups all-purpose flour

ONE OF THE advertising slogans that The Blues Bakery had was *Home of the Half-Pound Muffin*. That slogan was inaccurate in that each muffin weighed nine ounces, but accuracy lost out to the fact that half a pound sounds better than nine ounces. McDonald's calls its burger the Quarter Pounder, not the Four Ouncer.

The above recipe has been cut down from the commercial-sized batches of muffins made in Texas muffin tins, the large ones that created those nine-ounce muffins. The muffins that this recipe produces taste just as delicious but look less "oh my gosh!" They are, therefore, less filling and easier to consume by children and people with small appetites.

In other words, feel free to eat two.

Below this recipe is the one that will make six enormous, magnificent pumpkin muffins.

PREHEAT OVEN to 350

Melt the butter in a microwave and let it cool in the refrigerator, although the freezer is best, so long as you're paying attention. For the record, paying attention is generally a worthwhile practice, unless you're asked to sit through a ten-part Netflix mystery that could have made a decent movie but instead stumbles through the woods endlessly like a lost, drunken aardvark. In that case, time is better spent thinking about new quilt patterns or how to rearrange your kitchen utensils.

ADD COOLED butter to the eggs, sugar, and vanilla in a large mixing bowl.

Cream the above.

Add buttermilk, then mix.

Add cinnamon, cloves, salt, baking powder, and flour.

Mix until incorporated.

Spray a muffin tin with non-stick spray, or butter-and-flour the cups, or use paper muffin cups (you have a multitude of options, but if you choose to use none of the above and, therefore, a third of each muffin sticks to the tin, well, you only have yourself to blame, although how would I know if you blame your boss?).

Scoop enough batter into each cup so that a rounded crest protrudes slightly above each cup. I use an ice-cream scoop.

Bake for 32 minutes

Feel free to double the above recipe for 18 muffins or some additional multiple should you need to feed a horde.

For six enormous, magnificent pumpkin muffins made in Texas muffin tins:

5 1/2 ounces butter, about a stick and a half, melted and cooled

3 eggs

1 3/8 cups sugar

1/2 tsp vanilla

11 ounces pumpkin puree, about 3/4 of a 15 ounce can

1 scant cup low-fat buttermilk

1 TBL cinnamon

1 tsp cloves

A scant 1/2 tsp salt

1 3/4 TBLs baking powder

2 ½ cups all-purpose flour

Add cooled butter to the eggs, sugar, and vanilla in a large mixing bowl.

Cream the above.

Add buttermilk and pumpkin, then mix.

Add cinnamon, cloves, salt, baking powder, and flour.

Mix until incorporated.

Spray a muffin tin with non-stick spray, or butter-and-flour the cups, or use large paper muffin cups.

Scoop enough batter into each cup so that you ask, "Am I making muffins or mountains?" Settle for hills that crest well above the rims.

Bake for 42 minutes at 350

Tell yourself you've only eaten one muffin.

One 9-ounce muffin.

PUCKER-UP LEMON BARS

*M*akes 12 large bars

. . .

Suzanne Bigelow officially holds the title of McCracken County Attorney, although everyone calls her the D.A. (District Attorney) because we've all watched eighteen versions of *Law & Order* and other legal procedurals on television, and none of those shows calls the chief legal officer The Attorney.

Although she'll never name-drop her famous relative, Suzanne is two years older than her celebrity sister, Amanda Bigelow, the actress, heart-throb, and heartbreaker who lives in a mansion on the beach in Malibu.

I met Amanda and her hunky live-in partner at the time, Jack Drake, a private investigator, when I was beckoned to join a party being thrown by Amanda. I was walking along Broad Beach at dusk, when from one of the balconies of the architectural monstrosity that dangled from the steep slope above I heard, "Hey, you, lady. Wanna join the party?"

The woman's voice was familiar and sounded drunk. I looked up and saw Amanda Bigelow, whom I'd paid to see on the big screen many times, opening her arms to me, then gesturing toward the stairs that led from the beach up the side of her ghastly (okay, maybe gaudy is the more accurate word) mansion.

I didn't know why I was being summoned, and I worried as I walked past the kayaks hanging below the house, then figured out how to lower the steps to the beach, whether I was being lured, rather than invited. If a predator wanted to abduct a woman, he would be wise to use a gorgeous, familiar face to lower her defenses and encourage participation in whichever innocent endeavor was offered.

This is the wrong book in which to describe the "Hollywood" party I joined that night, but I will say that I enjoy Suzanne Bigelow's company far more than I do Amanda's. Amanda drinks as though Prohibition will start tomorrow, and Suzanne provided the following recipe for Pucker Up Lemon Bars, even though she's proprietary about them to the point of being self-righteous. But she let me include the recipe, so I'm grateful, as I am for most of my life these days.

. . .

PREHEAT OVEN to 300
    For the crust:
1/2 pound butter, melted
2 1/4 cups flour
1/2 cup plus 1 1/2 TBLs powdered sugar

FOR THE FILLING:
    Zest of two lemons
    4 eggs
    2 cups sugar
    1/4 cup flour
    1/3 cup plus 2 TBLs lemon juice
    1 tsp baking powder

MIX the still-hot butter with the 2 1/4 cups of flour and the powdered sugar until a ball forms.

Place the ball in the center of the pan, then use the heel of your hand and your fingers to spread the dough throughout the pan until it is very thin and reaches about three-quarters of an inch up the sides.

Tears and tears may occur. Repair the tears and dry the tears. Do not surrender to the impulse to quit before the tedious task is complete. Pretend you're quilting. Would you quit just because your seam allowances had flipped? No, you'd curse your fate, blame the cheap fabric or the phase of the moon, then correct the problem. As satisfying as putting the finishing touches on a gorgeous quilt is, the result definitely won't taste as great as these lemon bars will if you have enough patience to get the crust just so.

BAKE at 300 degrees for 20 minutes
While the crust is baking, break the eggs into a large mixing bowl, then add the 1/4 cup of flour, sugar, lemon zest, lemon juice, and baking powder. If you prepare the filling immediately after you put

the crust in to bake, be sure to zap the filling again with the mixer or to stir it well before the next step because the sugar settles and won't be evenly distributed.

CAREFULLY REMOVE the pan while wearing oven mitts, and set the pan on a flat surface, unless you are trying to sabotage this dessert because you prefer limes to lemons and can't understand how anyone could prefer such an inferior citrus. If spite is your motivation, feel free to set the pan on the floor and step on the crust with a hiking boot (or any other closed-toe footwear).

But if you'd rather make an excellent dessert, you should pour the filling into the crust slowly. The filling will find its level, and if you've created three-quarter-inch sides, that level should be near the top of the crust, without overflowing. If you have a little extra filling, the world won't end. Well, it may end, but I can guarantee that the extra filling will not be the cause of its demise.

INCREASE THE TEMPERATURE TO **325, then bake for 40 minutes**

Remove the pan. Now comes the nearly impossible part of this recipe—let the lemon bars cool to room temperature, then put them in the refrigerator for far too long.

Your friends and family who have smelled the wondrous aroma wafting through your home while the lemon bars have baked will question their friendships with you and maybe even their genetic links to you because of the cruelty you are displaying. You may have to grab a book, set a chair in front of the fridge, then physically prevent an assault on the not-ready-yet lemon bars.

You will, of course, have to summon willpower reserves that you didn't know you had because, after all, you are also human, and the scent of the baking lemon bars has tickled your olfactory nerve, too.

The next day—or, if mutiny is imminent after the threats of divorce didn't budge you—you can remove the lemon bars sooner and serve them to the impatient heathens.

I create twelve large lemon bars by setting the pan perpendicular to me, then carefully slicing down the middle of the pan. I cut each of those halves in half, then I rotate the pan and cut the length of the pan twice, more or less equally, creating twelve bars. People with more self-control than I have and those whose sugar consumption is being monitored should probably cut a bar in half.

I will admit that I have on occasion halved this recipe so that I didn't eat an entire pan within twenty-four hours. Have I downed a half-pan within that timeframe?

A woman never tells.

PURLOINED LEMON-POPPYSEED MUFFINS

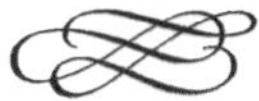

Makes 6 huge Texas-tin muffins

. . .

IN THE SMALL, locked chest of our mother's that my sister, Jenny, convinced me to open, I found a trove of information that dramatically improved my life, although it took many hours of rigorous effort for me to discover those improvements.

Attentive readers may discover in the previous sentence the makings of a plot that could find its way into a Hadley Carroll Mystery. Other readers who are driven by hunger and those who only read the bold text in cookbooks will likely skip this section, so the attentive readers among you should feel free to mull over possible plot points and to make fun of the readers who only read bold text.

Go ahead. Say what you must. Gossip is only rude if it's untrue. If you're simply recounting the fact that certain readers skip sections of books, then you're merely sharing a fact as documentarians do. However, gossip does become rude when gossipers use phrases such as "dumber than a no-brained nothing" or "amoeba seem like Einstein compared to those morons."

But I digress.

One of the many items I found in my mom's locked chest (I bought a bolt cutter at Harbor Freight to cut the padlock) sent ripples of shock through my system. Jenny and I were already stunned by the other contents of the chest, so I'd thought the chest had revealed its last surprise.

But the following recipe for lemon-poppyseed muffins was written on a notecard—in my handwriting.

As I sat with Jenny in my living room holding the notecard in my hand, I flashed on the day I'd written it. Bruce had just told me about the skinheads who had kicked a hole in the sandwich board his father had made (a blue guitar affixed to a white background) and thrown the tables and chairs in front of The Blues Bakery into the street earlier that morning. The glass tops on both tables had shattered, and Bruce had spent a long time making sure no shards were scattered in the street or hidden in the tables before he set them up again, without the glass tops sitting atop the painted wooden surfaces.

He'd sold out that morning of the other kinds of muffins, although it was only 9 a.m. (a church group had purchased three dozen muffins). While I waited for the next batch of pumpkin muffins to bake, Bruce said, "You told me last time that you don't like lemon poppyseed, but try this one."

I did, devoured it, then asked him for the recipe. He set a large blue notebook on the table next to me, and I copied the recipe onto a note-card. Later, I would make the conversions from the large batch and from the professional convection oven to my home oven.

However, I didn't make that conversion until now because for reasons beyond my understanding, the notecard with the recipe on it had been inside my mom's locked chest.

This may not seem all that strange to people who come from families that interact with each other regularly. Possessions get borrowed, stuff intermingles, and junk never quite makes it to the intended dumpster.

But between the day I left for college and the day I arrived again in Kentucky to take care of my dying mother, I hadn't seen her. In fact, we hadn't spoken for more than twelve years.

So, how did the recipe end up in her chest, which I broke into an additional twelve years later? I'd written that recipe when I was 2o, and as I write this I'm 42.

After staring dumbfounded at my handwriting on the card, I asked Jenny, "Did you send this to mom?"

"Don't think so. Only things I filched from you when I visited were the peach Banana Republic blouse—"

"That's where that went? I tore my apartment apart looking for it. Thanks, Jenny. Hope you enjoyed it."

"It was too big."

"Kind of deserved that, didn't you? What else did you take?"

"A ring, the one Dakota gave you."

"That's all? The only things you stole from me after I flew you to LA were my favorite blouse and the ring my best friend gave me? If I'd realized the ring was missing sooner, I would have figured out you'd taken it. But it gave me a rash, so I hadn't worn it in a while. When I went to look for it, I figured one of Danny's moron friends must've taken it, and I suspected his sister of stealing the blouse. Glad I didn't confront him or accuse her."

"I'm sorry, Hads. Really. If it makes you feel any better, the ring gave me a rash, too." I gave her a hug and thought, "You can't choose your family."

My best guess is that my mom must've tracked a friend or a boyfriend of mine down, then asked for one of the more bizarre favors ever: "Could you search Hadley's stuff, then send me the lemon-poppyseed recipe?" Knowing my mom, she would have added, "It's mine. I just asked her to write it out for me." But how would she have known about it? She couldn't have.

The other option—that my mom traveled from Paducah or Calvert City to LA, or Nashville, or … wait.

When I lived in Lexington and worked for the *Herald-Leader*, my apartment was burglarized. Everything that could be sold to a pawn-shop or on Craigslist or Facebook Marketplace had been stolen: my television, stereo, jewelry, camera, guitar, first-edition books, and most of my clothes. I'd thought it odd that a picture of Jenny and me when we were kids went missing, but I'd thought it had to have been broken while they ransacked the apartment, then been tossed by one of the friends who'd helped me clean up.

Could my mother have stolen the lemon-poppyseed muffin recipe while converting my possessions into booze and rent money?

I wouldn't put it past her.

But I'm grateful she kept it because now I can present it to you.

PREHEAT OVEN to 350
    1/3 pound butter (5.33 ounces), melted and cooled
    3 eggs
    1/4 cup lemon juice
    1/2 tsp vanilla
    1 TBL lemon zest
    1 1/8 cups sugar
    1 1/8 cups low-fat buttermilk

2 TBLs poppyseeds
1/2 tsp salt
2 TBLs baking powder
1/2 tsp baking soda
3 1/2 cups flour

CRACK the three eggs into a large mixing bowl. Add the cooled butter, lemon juice, vanilla, and zest, then blend thoroughly.

If you care deeply about aesthetics, you may want to add two drops of yellow food coloring. I am not so uptight … I mean, I don't care so deeply about aesthetics. But do whatever makes you happy. This is a cookbook, not your taxes.

Add the poppyseeds, salt, baking powder, baking soda, and flour, then mix until incorporated.

Scoop the batter evenly into well-greased or sprayed Texas tins, then **bake at 350 for 40 minutes**.

You can buy the large tins on Amazon and elsewhere. Or you can use regular-sized tins, disappoint residents of the Lone Star State, then adjust the time down to about 32 minutes, but use a toothpick to check whether they're done.

And don't steal from your sister or daughter.

QUICK CANNOLI

$\mathcal{M}$akes 8 servings

. . . .

I DON'T CARE whether you say "a cannoli," rather than "a cannolo," as the Italian language dictates, just as I don't care whether you say "a graffiti," rather than "a graffito."

But I do care if you say, "I'd like two cannolis, please." The word cannoli is plural, so therefore the S is unnecessary. Don't ask me why both inaccuracies don't bother me equally because I won't be able to answer, and I'm known for my snappy retorts.

Should *you* care that *I* care about these trivial grammatical concerns? Absolutely not. Pronounce the above words however you'd like because it is my job to provide you with recipes and perhaps some laughs. It is not my job to police your grammar or to limit the number of cannoli you consume in one sitting, or while standing at the sink in your undergarments.

Or maybe that's just me.

I ate cannoli (yes, I ate more than one) for the first time in a glitzy bakery in New York City's Greenwich Village. I had scrimped and saved so I could see theater on Broadway. I saw four shows (after buying discount tickets at TKTS in Times Square). I loved three of them and wondered, while struggling to sit through the fourth, why I'd spent so much money to watch what was basically a television sitcom.

After enjoying one of the shows, I visited The Village, as it's called locally, saw a dessert I'd never seen, purchased one, devoured it, purchased another, tried but failed to eat it more slowly, then had the audacity to ask the clerk what was in these magical cannoli.

I tried not to look like a total rube by letting my jaw drop when he told me, "Our special combination of ricotta and mascarpone, sweetheart." I let the old guy get away with the overly familiar, borderline sexist comment because I had no idea that the two confections I'd just eaten had been filled with cheese. He wouldn't even hint at how he made the scrumptious, delicious shell that contained the cheese. I said, "That's okay, darling. They were delicious. Thank you."

Should you find yourself compelled to make cannoli from scratch (as I've done), you'll find dozens of recipes online that will suggest which kinds of shaping dowels, piping bags, and piping tips you should purchase, then tell you how best to heat the oil, fry the shells, retrieve them without burning yourself, then pipe in the filling that you may have chosen to supplement with chocolate chips, pistachio nuts, or slivers of fruit.

I am not here to prevent you from pursuing your goal of making cannoli from scratch.

I am, however, here to suggest that you can save ALL of the hassle but still retain 87.4 percent of the cannoli experience by making the filling from scratch, then filling waffle cones with it.

Yes, I understand that many of you cannot read this sentence because you've smashed your tablet against the counter, thrown your phone across the room, or set the paperback edition on fire.

Culinary purists have just written me out of their wills, and I may never be allowed in Italy. But if that's the price I must pay to save you time, effort, and money, then I can live with that, so long as you invite me over when you make quick cannoli.

2 15-OUNCE CONTAINERS of whole milk ricotta (if you'd like to substitute some portion of mascarpone, feel free)

1 10-ounce package of semi-sweet mini morsels, separated into two portions

3/4 cup powdered sugar

1 tsp vanilla extract

1/2 tsp vanilla paste (if you don't have it, double the vanilla extract)

8 waffle cones

PREFERABLY USING A DOUBLE BOILER, melt half of the chocolate (if you use a microwave, only you and your conscience will know). When the chocolate is melted, dip the wide ends of the cones into the chocolate, then by whichever method you deem effective (I use the back of a teaspoon), spread chocolate in the insides of the cones, at least an inch down from the top. Let the chocolate set. I place the cones in coffee cups to contain the creep of chocolate around my kitchen.

By the way, during this step, I keep Trapunto in the back yard. He has proven faster and I clumsier than I would like.

In a large mixing bowl, fold the ricotta, powdered sugar, vanilla, and vanilla paste together with a wooden spoon or a spatula of whichever color you prefer.

Some people insist that the ricotta should have been drained overnight, sitting in the fridge in a strainer, barely releasing any liquid. Preparing one's cheese that way is fine, but those people stopped reading this cookbook long ago because they are in Italy buying ricotta and mascarpone from an artisan named Enrico who wouldn't be caught dead watching a television cooking show, let alone using waffle cones instead of cannoli shells made from scratch—as if there is any other kind.

Add about half of the chocolate chips, erring toward too few, rather than too many. You can always add more if you don't think the proportions look right.

If you have more patience than I do, you should set the bowl containing the filling in the freezer for a few minutes or in the refrigerator for fifteen. As you may have guessed from the previous sentence, I skip this step.

Leaving the piping set in the drawer where it likely has sat undisturbed since just after it was given to you as a gift, spoon the filling into the cones.

Dig in.

The time and energy you saved by making Quick Cannoli can be used to work off the calories you just consumed by working out, cleaning house, tidying up the yard, or ... making Butternut Beauties or Magnificent Mocha Panna Cotta, if you haven't already.

If you're busy making those, this sentence is unnecessary. However, as some of you smart-aleck readers have already concluded, so are all of them in this book. I mean, does the world really need another cookbook or three-hundred and eight?

After I complete this sentence, I will devour the last two quick cannoli, so the answer—to me—is yes.

SCRUMPTIOUS LEMON-PECAN SCONES

$\mathcal{M}$akes 10 scones

· · ·

I WAS SORTING my bits and bobs while summering in Sussex on an estate owned by Prince William when his butler, Alfred, asked me how I "took" my scone.

Although the man-servant was smartly dressed and had impeccable diction, I believed his question to be impertinent because he assumed I knew what a scone was. Feeling the sting of his presumptuousness but not wanting to make a scene, I set my teacup in its saucer, stiffened my upper lip, stood, fled the drawing room without an utterance, then filled the void inside me with a pint at the local pub, The Tall Tale.

Okay, I've never been to Sussex, met Prince William, spoken to a man-servant, nor been subjected to a non-existent man-servant's impertinence.

But if I'd told you I was reading a cookbook, scanned a recipe for raisin scones, and decided I could create a more inspired (and probably more delicious) recipe, would that have been an acceptable beginning? Maybe. But I'm confident it's an acceptable fourth paragraph.

PREHEAT OVEN **to 400**

> **2 cups flour**
> **1/4 cup sugar**
> **1 TBL grated lemon zest**
> **2 tsps baking powder**
> **1/2 tsp baking soda**
> **1/4 tsp salt**
> **1/2 cup Crisco**
> **1 cup pecans, chopped**
> **1/2 cup milk, plus 1 TBL**
> **2 tsps vanilla extract**

IN A LARGE MIXING BOWL, mix the flour, sugar, lemon zest, baking powder, baking soda, and salt.

Using whichever method you prefer to cut the Crisco into the dry ingredients (unless you use eyebrow tweezers, in which case we have a problem), cut the Crisco into the flour mixture. I use a pastry blender because I'm not insane. Of course, insane people almost never admit they are mentally unwell, so perhaps I'm the one doing it wrong, and using eyebrow tweezers really is the way to go.

You're not trying to turn the mixture into a fine powder—a coarse crumb is what you want. When you've accomplished this objective, add the pecans, then mix.

Add the milk and the vanilla, then mix. Ask yourself which Golden Girl made the show pop. Don't spend too long thinking about it because the answer is Betty White. If you think it was Rue McClanahan, then you probably won't like these scones.

Flour a cutting board or another work surface that your cats haven't recently reclined on.

When the dough comes together, separate it into two equal sections. Form balls out of each. Pat them into disks about six- or seven inches across. Cut them into wedges of relatively equal size, unless you have a grudge against Alfred, the butler, in which case you should give him the smallest wedge.

Some people would feel inclined to create six or eight small wedges, but I prefer the scones to look like scones and not arrowheads, so I go with five. That way, when I eat all of them, I've only eaten five scones, not six or eight.

Again, the ability to rationalize is underrated.

BAKE at 400 on an ungreased cookie sheet for 15 minutes
Eat them plain or slather them with butter, jelly, or clotted cream.
How does it feel to be genteel?

*M*akes 1 loaf

. . .

THIS IS my spin on pound cake. However, because we don't need to be reminded of weights and measures while indulging in desserts, I've reconfigured and renamed this delectable.

It has the same amount of fat, sugar, and calories that it would have if I called it pound cake, but it is less-sweet and more spicy than traditional pound cake, so that should count for something, if we abandon our definition of what matters.

It's been said that lowering our expectations is the key to happiness, but whichever blowhard spewed that hogwash hadn't tasted this cake.

Instead of lowering your standards, learn to rationalize.

Sure, you could exercise off the extra bulk you're about to add— and I'm not arguing against doing so—but rationalizing can be done anywhere and in any weather, plus it's gluten- and calorie free.

In other words, have another slice.

PREHEAT OVEN to 350

1/4 CUP **milk**

   4 egg whites

   1 TBL vanilla extract

   2 sticks butter (8 ounces), softened

   2 cups flour, preferably cake flour, but now is not the time to stand on ceremony, not with all the nonsense going on in the world. I'm not saying you should become a shut-in to avoid the tumult roiling beyond your kitchen, but if you do, at least this cake should bring you some joy. In other words, use all-purpose flour if that's what you have.

   3/4 cup sugar

   1 tsp baking powder

   1 tsp cinnamon

   3/4 tsp cloves

   2 tsps cocoa powder, unsweetened

. . .

GREASE AND FLOUR A LOAF PAN, then line it with parchment paper. I never thought I'd write that sentence. I am simply not a parchment girl. Or I never used to be. But one time I followed the directions that used parchment paper just so I could prove the author wrong, but I was the one proven wrong, and I became a parchment believer. It's a thing. You can look it up.

Combine the milk, egg whites and vanilla, swirling in a figure-eight pattern with the handle of a ball-peen hammer. Kidding. Obviously, you should use the metal side. Fine, use a spatula if you prefer, just so long as you mix the ingredients adequately.

In a large bowl, combine the flour, sugar, baking powder, cinnamon, cloves, and cocoa, sifting with your grandmother's garden trowel.

It's the same joke, people—only the implement has changed.

Now that you've sifted the dry ingredients and I got that sophomoric comedy out of my system, add the butter to the dry ingredients, then add the egg mixture, a little at a time, mixing as you go. Scrape down the sides, then continue to beat air into the mixture for precisely 67 seconds. Or you could go with a minute, if you're in a hurry.

Pour, scrape, maneuver, coax, and cajole the batter into the lined pan. Level it with your ball peen (sorry, but I think I'm coming down with something), then **bake it at 350 for 45 minutes**.

Loaf pans come in different sizes and can be made of different materials. My loaf, baked in a long, thin aluminum pan, turned out perfectly after 45 minutes. Yours may require more or less.

Which is true of most things.

Except rationalizing.

Always more.

THANK YOU, HONEY, WHEAT BREAD

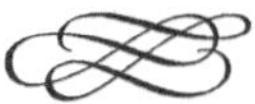

*S*erves however many

. . .

IN ADDITION to my addictions to quilting and coffee, I'm addicted to starches: pasta, rice, potatoes, and bread, bread, bread.

If I could only indulge in one of those items for the rest of my life, I'd choose the middle bread, provided it was a true baguette from a French patisserie, a boule of sourdough from Fishermen's Wharf in San Francisco, an Olive Loaf from Kirchhoff's Bakery & Deli in Paducah, or this loaf, which I just named Thank you, Honey, Wheat Bread.

I couldn't just call it Wheat Bread without questioning who I've become, but I couldn't come up with anything clever, so I went with what I went with, and I'm going to have to live with it—unless I decide to change it by the time I finish writing this entry, or at an indeterminate time in the future, because technology allows me to do that, and I'm entitled to change my mind.

And to write unwieldy sentences, apparently. Or maybe not.

Be honest: How long ago did you stop reading this section? Wow, that far back? I thought the picture would have held your attention longer than that. Wait, what? You've returned this book and bought one by Giada De Laurentiis? Well, she sure knows what she's doing in the kitchen, and she's gorgeous, so good for you.

But if you've already returned this book, and, therefore, aren't reading this, then I'll tell the readers who have stuck with me that it's a shame that crustaceans had to die for your mediocre crab cakes, and your paper piecing ... well, I'll just leave that comment unsaid.

But I will tell the rest of you how to make this bread.

1 1/2 tsps yeast
   3 TBLs warm water
   4 cups whole wheat flour
   1 cup all-purpose flour
   1 1/2 tsps salt
   1/4 cup honey
   1 3/4 cups water, plus one tablespoon
   1 tablespoon olive oil

. . .

DISSOLVE the yeast in a large mixing bowl with the warm water. Swirl until dissolved. Speed the process along with your fingers, if you must, or with the back of a spoon.

Add both kinds of flour, the salt, honey, and 1 3/4 cups of water. I bring the mixture together with a wooden spoon, but a dough hook on a hand-mixer or one of those fancy tabletop models that are the envy of financially struggling, quilting journalists everywhere will work, too.

When it seems as though the dough will not come together, I add the last tablespoon of water, and, *voila!*

Kneed the dough by hand or with your fancy mixer for a few minutes.

Add the olive oil to a bowl large enough to hold the dough while it rises. Coat the dough in the olive oil, then cover the bowl and let the dough proof for at least an hour and a half. I prefer two, which allows me more time to quilt while trying not to be distracted by how much I'm going to enjoy eating the bread if it ever hurries up and presents itself to me.

PREHEAT the oven to 425

Put a Dutch oven or another heavy-duty pot in the oven with the lid on while the oven gets up to temp.

Carefully remove the pot using oven mitts, set it on the stove or the counter (if your counters are built to handle hot pots), remove the lid, then transfer the dough into the sizzling pot.

I gently tug around the edges of the dough, kind of freeing it from the bowl, then invert the bowl over the pot, letting gravity transfer the dough so I'm in no danger of touching the pot.

Put the oven mitts back on, put the lid on the pot, then transfer to the middle rack of the over.

Bake at 425 with the lid on for 30 minutes

. . .

Remembering to use oven mitts, carefully remove the top and set it on the stove. Close the oven door and **bake the bread for another ten minutes, making 40 minutes total**.

Carefully remove the pot, remove the lid, then invert the loaf into your oven-mitted hand, then set the dark-but-not-burned loaf on a cooling rack until it is safe to touch and consume. If you want to transfer the loaf from the pot directly to the cooling rack, that's your choice.

If you want to use the resulting loaf as a pillow—after it cools down, of course—that, too, is your right because this is a free country, and nothing in this cookbook is either mandated by nor specifically restricted by the Constitution of the United States of America. So, if you have to pillow, pillow.

The rest of us will eat our warm bread in whichever manner we find the most delectable. I prefer to dip mine in olive oil, a habit I picked up from a certain tall, dark, and handsome man.

WHO KNEW? CHOCOLATE CHIP MUFFINS

*M*akes about a dozen

. . . .

THOSE OF YOU who have been paying attention (don't worry—there won't be a test at the end of this book) will notice that the basic recipe that follows is the same as the one for Bluesberry Muffins. In fact, even if you haven't been paying attention or haven't looked at the other recipe, you now know it's the same because I've just let you in on that non-secret.

I invented this recipe on the fly when I realized my beloved and I had eaten the last of the frozen blueberries the night before. I hadn't set out all of the necessary ingredients before I started to bake as some people feel compelled to do.

You know who you are, and I'm not judging. But if I were the kind of woman who sets out all of her ingredients before I start, then this recipe wouldn't exist, which pretty much slams the door on meticulous organization—unless someone is trying to solve murders, in which case hyper-meticulous organization is necessary. Or so I've heard.

If Bruce had sold Who Knew? Chocolate Chip Muffins in The Blues Bakery, his bottom-line would certainly have been better. However, the tendonitis in both wrists that he developed because of the repetitive nature of the work and the extremely long hours he put in would still have hobbled him, so if he'd sold these muffins, he still would have had to sell the bakery but at a better price.

He wouldn't have objected to that financial development, of course, but he was about ready to move on, independent of his health, because he believed he had a novel or ten in him that needed to be written and read. But working seven days a week, including occasional sixteen-hour days, running a small business and making and selling baked goods, however tasty, was not conducive to crafting plots, fleshing out characters, and obsessing over sentences.

In other words, it's lucky for all of us that Bruce has inferior tendons.

PREHEAT OVEN to 350

A stick and a half of butter (3/4 of a cup), melted, then cooled
3 eggs
1 1/4 cups sugar
1/2 tsp vanilla
1 1/8 cups low-fat buttermilk
1/2 tsp salt
2 TBLs baking powder
3 1/2 cups flour
1 1/4 cups chocolate chips

CRACK THREE EGGS INTO A LARGE, empty mixing bowl.

Add sugar, vanilla, and cooled butter.

Cream.

Add buttermilk, then mix.

Add salt, baking powder, and flour.

Mix until incorporated.

Add the chocolate chips. I prefer semi-sweet, but what I prefer isn't really relevant unless you intend to invite me over for dessert.

If you do, I appreciate the gesture, truly, but I feel compelled to remind you that I'm a character in a cozy mystery series, so setting a place at your table for me will likely result in your family exchanging knowing looks with each other, then expressing concern for you as they wonder whether to seek medical assistance.

If you've successfully negotiated that digression, line the muffin tins with paper muffin cups, or grease them, flour them, and remove the excess flour, then scoop with whichever utensil pleases you (if you choose a fork, perhaps you should leave the baking to others), until the cups are between heaping and overflowing.

BAKE at 350 for 32 minutes

If y'all are unsure (let's face it, we are all unsure from time to time, and many of us are all of the time), insert a toothpick into a muffin. If it comes out dry (other than melted chocolate), let them cool, then dig in. If it's wet (with batter), leave the muffins in for another minute or two.

Occasionally, running out of frozen blueberries can be advantageous, but I do my best not to make a habit of it.

SAVORY

BRANDON'S CLAMS AND LINGUINE

*S*erves 3 or 4

. . .

I EXPECTED to be far more nervous than I turned out to be when Hadley arrived at my door, ready to sample my cooking for the first time. Of course, she'd been on my mind for nearly a year and a half, and I'd waited patiently for her to feel comfortable enough with herself and with having lost Matt to date again.

And when she was ready, she chose to date me. It's fair to say our first date turned out to be far more exciting than a first date should be, and our second date didn't end on the high note that either of us had hoped it would, due to dire circumstances outside our control. I'm sure you noticed the vagueness in those sentences, but not everyone has read *Quilt City: Panic in Paducah* yet, and this is a cookbook, not a spoiler of mystery plots.

That said, the meal I prepared for Hadley is below.

1 POUND **dry linguine**
   3 cans chopped clams
   3 TBLs extra-virgin olive oil, plus a splash
   2 TBLs butter
   2 or 3 garlic cloves, minced, depending on garlic fondness
   The juice of 1 1/2 or 2 lemons, to taste
   1/2 cup parsley
   Salt
   Black pepper
   Red pepper flakes

FILL a large pot with at least four quarts of water. Add a handful of salt. I also add a splash of olive oil. Bring to a boil.

While the water is heating, pour the olive oil and drop the butter into a large frying pan. When the butter has melted, add the garlic, stirring occasionally.

When the water boils, add the linguine (when I've been out of linguine, I've made this with other pastas, and the dish still tastes great), being sure to push all of it beneath the surface, then stirring frequently.

Add the clams to the frying pan, then add about a third of the chopped parsley, the salt, pepper, and red pepper flakes, to taste. I like my pasta spicy, so I add two or three shakes of the container. Squeeze the juice of one lemon into the frying pan, then stir.

When the pasta is al dente, meaning about eleven or twelve minutes (carefully taste a strand, but it will be very hot), turn off the heat and pour the water and pasta into a colander in the sink, being careful to avoid the steam. Shake the colander to drain the water.

Transfer the pasta into individual dishes or a large bowl, then pour the clam sauce over the top. I find it easier to integrate the sauce when I use a large bowl, then transfer the content to serving bowls.

Add the juice of the remaining half a lemon or whole lemon, then the rest of the parsley.

Serve with some fava beans and a nice chianti.

I didn't want to write that line, but Hadley's standing over my shoulder. She's the writer, and she suggested it. I apologize for the stale joke, but I'm just here for her peanut butter cookies.

Although she professes not to be a violent person, that last line elicited a smack on my arm.

It was worth it.

CINDY'S WONTON SOUP

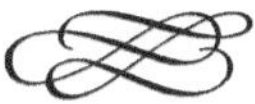

*M*akes 2 servings

. . .

CINDY BARON, a Paducah Quilters Quorum member, is kind and generous, has a lovely smile and a beautiful singing voice, and once created a small Moon Over the Mountain quilt blindfolded to prove her husband wrong. He was so critical of her talents that he promised her a Royal Caribbean cruise to the Bahamas if she could create the quilt.

"I'll accept the challenge," she'd said, "but only if I get to go alone. All you'd do is complain and say you were missing this game or that game, then you'd find fault with everything and everyone."

"You got a deal," Ned had said. "Who'd want to eat that slop, sleep in a shoebox, be pestered to do all kinds of stupid stuff I'd never do at home, and get seasick, all while paying for it and missing the bowl games?"

The quilt took her longer than she thought it would, and it wouldn't have won a blue ribbon if she'd made it without having been blindfolded, but it was passable and plenty good enough to win the bet.

Cindy has many talents, but she used to underestimate her kitchen skills. Straight-ahead meat-and-potatoes bumped up against her culinary limits. But that cruise changed her.

Just after returning from an excursion to Atlantis Bahamas, a fancy resort, Cindy sat next to a woman in the dining room from San Francisco, California, who eventually provided Cindy with the following recipe for wonton soup.

Cindy's confidence soared when she returned home and was able to produce a dish that turned out to be far more tasty than she'd anticipated it would be—and far better than any other meal she'd made.

Ned's response to the soup was, "I knew I shouldn't'a sent you on that cruise. I like food, not this nonsense."

Cindy is now an accomplished cook, and she is happily remarried.

* * *

THE FILLING BELOW is enough to fill approximately one package of wanton skins (50). The broth that follows will accommodate half of those wantons, which means you can either freeze half of the wantons to use in another meal, or you can double the broth if you have a very large pot or have two large pots.

I used a 5-quart pot to make 25 wantons using the recipe below for the broth.

FOR THE FILLING:
   1 pound ground pork
   1 1/2 TBLs grated ginger
   2 TBLs aji-mirin cooking rice seasoning
   1 TBL soy sauce
   2 TBLs sesame oil
   2 scallions, thinly sliced, reserving about a quarter of the slices
   1/2 tsp black pepper
   1/4 tsp salt
   1 package of wonton wrappers

FOR THE BROTH:
   2 large garlic cloves, lightly crushed
   2 thick slices ginger
   4 cups chicken stock, bone broth, or vegetable broth (those with certain health conditions may want to consider low-sodium options)
   1 1/2 TBLs soy sauce
   2 TBLs aji-mirin cooking rice seasoning
   1 cup sliced mushrooms
   2 handfuls spinach leaves, coarsely chopped

MIX all of the ingredients for the filling, except the wonton wrappers, in a large bowl. If you have a stand mixer, use the paddle attachment and mix for about a minute.

Wontons can be made with various techniques and in various shapes. I wet my index finger in a bowl filled with water, then wet the four edges of the wanton wrappers. Others wet a small culinary brush, then apply water to the edges. The easiest shape is the triangle, although these will not freeze as well as the other shapes.

Place about a rounded half-teaspoon of filling in the middle of the wrapper. Wet the edges. Bring one corner across the wrapper to meet the far corner, creating a triangle. Carefully seal the edges, being sure to pinch any air from within. If you're not adept at the pinching process, you can decrease the likelihood that the wonton will come apart by piercing the wrapper with a fork.

The second shape is called the flower bud. Using the triangle you've created, roll the wrapped filling toward the single point of the triangle, then wrap the other two points around each other and press them together.

The third shape is called a nurse cap. Instead of creating a triangle, create a rectangle, seal it well, then bring the two corners that you've just created together and press hard, sealing them.

You may choose to shape a few of each to see which one you prefer. They'll all taste the same.

ADD THE BROTH, garlic cloves, ginger slices, soy sauce, and aji-mirin to a large pot, then bring to a boil.

Turn down the heat a little and add 25 wantons, the mushrooms, and spinach.

Cook for 4 minutes

Ladle into bowls, add a splash of sesame oil and more scallion slices to each bowl, then enjoy.

EASY-PEASY SALAD

S erves 4 or 5

. . .

Before my fellow PQQ members conferred on me full-time baker status for our Sunday quilting sessions, I did my best to deliver a range of savory dishes, instead of bringing along the same go-to dish every week, unlike a certain PQQer whose roasted potatoes are delicious, but do they go with pizza or pasta?

Because I'd worked almost throughout the night to meet a deadline on a long investigative article I wrote, I was running late one Sunday a few years ago. I didn't have time to go to the store, return, then cook a hot meal, so I looked in my refrigerator and cupboards, got creative, and the Easy Peasy Salad introduced itself to the world (or at least to PQQ, which, in a certain light, at least for a couple of us, *is* the world). I've made upgrades since that first version, and I'll probably continue to do so.

For today, however, the recipe is as follows:

1 pound to 1 1/2 pounds small tomatoes, such as cherry or grape. If you'd prefer to cut them in half so a streak of tomato juice doesn't shoot out of your mouth every time you bite into one, you should probably do so.

It's been said that knowledge is knowing that tomatoes are fruit, but wisdom is knowing not to include them in a fruit salad.

It's also been said that "if" is the middle word in "life," which leaves "le" as the outer word. That's fine if you speak French, but the rest of us are stuck guessing, "le what?"

Lemon? Leopard? Lepidopterophobia?

Never mind.

1 can black olives, pitted, preferably California olives
    1 can great northern beans, drained and rinsed
    1 12-ounce jar marinated, quartered artichoke hearts
    1/3 cup olive oil
    2 TBLs balsamic vinegar
    3 garlic cloves, pressed or minced

Chopped parsley, plenty
Salt
Pepper
Red pepper flakes
Italian seasoning, liberally distributed

I PREFER to mix the dressing first by blending the olive oil, vinegar, garlic, parsley, salt, pepper, red pepper flakes, and Italian seasoning.

I suggest cutting the quartered artichoke hearts in half and removing any hard, tough parts.

Place the tomatoes, olives, beans, and artichokes in a bowl, pour the dressing over the mixture, toss, then serve.

FISH STICKS & TATER TOTS

Follow the directions on the packages.

MIKE'S JAMBALAYA

*M*akes 5 or 6 servings

· · ·

I'll be cautious here so I don't spoil the plots of any of the Hadley Carroll Mysteries (two as I write this; more down the road, I hope, because I'd hate for this to be my swan song).

Mike Weiss is a lawyer in Paducah who specializes in contract law. I'd interviewed him once when I worked for the *Paducah Chronicle*, and he was bright and funny.

So, when I found myself "in a spot of bother,"—I wrote that in an English accent for reasons I don't understand—I called Mike. He implemented the lessons he learned at Harvard Law and honed during two decades of practice, and he won my civil suits.

One morning while riding my bike along the Greenway Trail, I saw Mike walking toward me. He wore a blue Nike sweatshirt, black sweatpants, and blue Nike running shoes. As I slowed down to say hello, I noticed he looked awful: sweating profusely and wearing a hang-dog expression, although he smiled when he looked up and saw me.

"Hadley! How's my favorite reporter?"

I stopped riding and said, "I'm fine, Mike. Are you okay? You don't look so good."

"Nothing awful. Bad but not awful."

"What's wrong?"

"Billy's been sick. The doctors don't know what it is. It looks like an autoimmune disease, but none of the specialists can pin it down. Janey and I are trying to put on a brave face, but we're frantic."

"Oh, I'm so sorry. Can I help in some way? Need me to cook or clean or have Laurel stay with me for a while? She's how old now, 12?"

"Just turned 13. She's kind of doing her own thing and doesn't realize how serious her brother's illness is, and Billy's handling it like a trooper. But Janey and I are exhausted. I think we've ordered pizza seven nights running because neither of us is sleeping, and we don't have the energy to cook and clean. I've put the practice on hold, but Janey can't take a leave from school without all kinds of hoops to jump through, and she doesn't want to turn over her kids mid-semester to a sub."

"Mike, I'm not just offering. I'd like to help. Would it be okay if I were to prepare a bunch of meals for y'all? I'm writing a cookbook, and I have to make the dishes anyway so I can photograph them. I can't eat everything I'm making, so I've been giving plate after plate to neighbors and friends. You and Janey are both, and you also have a real need for it right now."

"If you're serious, we'll take you up on it. This is the first time I've done anything resembling exercise—worrying isn't aerobic, I've learned—in nearly two months."

"I didn't know y'all were going through this. I would've helped earlier."

"You're helping now, and we really appreciate it. We'll reimburse you, of course."

"You can try, anyway. Unless a huge breaking news story happens as I'm leaving the office tonight, I should be able to deliver y'all something by seven. Is that too late?"

"That will be perfect. Billy and I should be back from Nashville by then. Seeing yet another specialist."

"Good luck, and I'll see you tonight."

* * *

THE DOCTORS never figured out which autoimmune disease had debilitated Billy to the extent that he'd had to quit the baseball team and be homeschooled by Mike and Janey. He would lay on his bed in a ball, holding his gut and writhing in pain. About half of his hair fell out, and the bottoms of his feet alternated between tingling or feeling like his skin was four sizes too small.

Three and a half weeks after I started preparing meals for the Weiss family, Billy's symptoms began to disappear. A week later, he was back to his vibrant 16-year-old self. The doctors were baffled, and Billy was written up in a couple of medical journals.

I'm not saying my food had anything to do with Billy's recovery.

But I'm not saying it didn't.

As a show of gratitude, Mike and Janey said they'd buy me a plane ticket to anywhere in the United States I wanted to go and pay for a stay in a nice hotel. I thanked them and said I'd gladly help them again for free, so I wouldn't accept the ticket.

"Hadley," Mike said, "I know your background, so I understand this is difficult for you. But healthy people let other people help them, and friendships are allowed to work in both directions. You helped us tremendously. Your food was delicious, and after the third day, Billy started to ask what you'd be bringing that night. I'm not saying that eating far too many sweets cured him, but I think having something to look forward to certainly helped. So, please accept our gratitude and the trip."

"You're right. That was rude of me. I'm sorry. If your offer is open-ended, then I'll gladly accept it. Thank you."

"It is. And there's something else I'd like to give you: a recipe. You wouldn't know it because I'm a Jew in Paducah, but my mama was Cajun, God rest her soul. She taught me how to make jambalaya. Every family does it a little differently, but I've always been fond of the way the Guidry's make ours, and I'd like you to have the recipe."

"That's tremendous. If you're comfortable with letting the four readers who are likely to buy the cookbook peer into the Guidry's kitchen, then of course I'd love to include it."

"It's all yours, and *laissez les bon temps rouler.*"

"That's not my strong suit, but I promise to try."

I present to you Mike's Masterful Jambalaya:

Spice mix:

  ½ tsp black pepper

  ½ tsp white pepper

  ½ tsp red pepper

  ½ tsp smoked paprika

  1 tsp filé powder (it's in most grocery stores in the South, but if you're elsewhere, you may have to search)

  1 tsp dry mustard powder

  ½ tsp cumin

  ½ tsp thyme

2 bay leaves

½ to 1 tsp salt (1 if you want it to taste good; ½ if you're trying to cut back on salt)

VEGGIES:

1 onion, chopped (should be about 2 cups)

1 celery heart, chopped (should be about 2 cups)

1 bell pepper, chopped (should be about 1 1/2 cups)

4 large or 6 medium garlic cloves, minced

MEAT:

4 boneless, skinless chicken thighs, cut in big chunks

2 links Aidell's andouille sausage, cut in half lengthwise, and then sliced into pieces about ¼ inch thick

3/4 pound shrimp (the weight after peeling and deveining)

OTHER INGREDIENTS:

½ stick butter

2 ¼ cups converted rice (or regular long grain, but not minute rice)

3 cups chicken stock (I prefer Kitchen Basics or homemade)

1 14-ounce can diced tomatoes (or 2 cups diced fresh tomatoes if you have some good homegrown ones)

PREHEAT OVEN to 350

In a heavy, lidded Dutch oven (a Le Creuset if cooking at Dakota's house), melt the butter and brown the andouille. While the sausage is browning, chop the vegetables.

When the sausage is rendered of most fat and getting crispy around the edges, add the vegetables.

Scrape down the bottom of the pot well after the veggies start to weep their juice. Sauté for about 5 minutes, then add the spice mixture and sauté for another 5 minutes.

Add the chicken chunks and cook down another 5 minutes.

Add the stock, tomatoes, and rice, then put the lid on and **bake at 350 for 30 minutes**.

After 30 minutes, add the shrimp. Just poke the shrimp down into the jambalaya with a wooden spoon, or a silicone spatula, or a metal one. Or you can use a cricket bat that you whittled into the shape of a swan and tried to sell on eBay, but no one met your minimum bid.

It's probably better to use a wooden spoon.

Bake for about 5 minutes more. If you're serving this at a buffet or potluck and want to make sure someone like Garrett Hunt (love you, Garrett, I do, but you're a man of appetites, and that's the most polite way I can put it) doesn't accidentally-on-purpose extract a disproportionate number of shrimp in his serving, cut each shrimp in half before adding. Doing so will allow more people to partake of the shrimp.

Turn the oven off. The jambalaya will taste better if it rests a while before serving, so I usually either let the dish stand in the cooling oven or on the counter for about 15 minutes.

This recipe isn't crazy hot, but it's hot enough. It's already less hot than how most Louisiana cooks would make it, but if you have to go easier on the heat, cut back equally on the black, white, and red pepper, and leave the other spices the same.

LET THE GOOD TIMES ROLL.

MRS. V'S STUFFED SHELLS

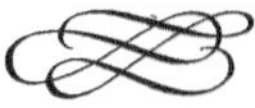

*S*erves 6 or more

. . .

TWO DAYS after our mom took us to Cracker Barrel for Jenny's eighth birthday, Ellen Carroll picked up a guy in Roof Brothers Wine & Liquor, and they drove to Dayton, Ohio together in his Cutlass Supreme.

Jenny and I didn't know any of this at the time, of course. All we knew was that our mother didn't return from the errand she said she had to run.

By then I understood that "running an errand" meant buying alcohol. When we needed groceries, she'd say, "Goin' to Kroger. Don't y'all give me no reason to beat you when I get back." But when she said, "Gotta run a errand," we knew we were far more likely to get hit when she returned.

Jenny took to waiting about fifteen minutes after Mom left for the liquor store before she climbed into bed and waited for the front door to open. When she heard Mom enter, she'd pretend she was asleep, on the theory that Mom wouldn't wake her up just to hit her. It worked most of the time.

About two hours later that Saturday afternoon, we were lucky—if I can put such a rose-tinted spin on being abandoned again—when our neighbor, Dolores Veneziale knocked on our door to see if we wanted to join her and her three daughters for stuffed shells. I didn't know what they were and was almost certain Jenny wouldn't like them because she hated almost everything that wasn't peanut butter and jelly, pizza, or cereal.

I didn't have the guts to ask Mrs. Veneziale if she'd seen our mom leave, but I suspected she had because she'd never stopped by to offer us food when Mom was home.

It turned out that stuffed shells were, in fact, pasta, rather than the seafood I expected, and even Jenny loved them. I thought they were a whole new kind of delicious. If this was Italian food, then which nation did those soggy discs Domino's sells come from?

Mrs. Veneziale insisted we stay with her family, so we did for the next six days. Jenny and I felt like we were on the best vacation anyone had ever experienced. We received three delicious meals a day and as many snacks as we wanted. No one shouted at each other, and the three daughters—twins Valerie and Veronica, and eldest sister, Barbara, all teenagers—interacted with their parents in a way Jenny and I never had with Mom. I didn't see fear, disappointment, and resentment on their faces but affection, admiration, and love.

This is the first time I've mentioned this to anyone, including my therapist, but on day three of our vacation in the apartment three doors away I wished Mom wouldn't make it home. I didn't want her to die, but I wanted more of what we were experiencing because we were being treated so well, so lovingly, by people who were not much more than strangers. If Mom found somewhere else to be miserable, I wouldn't have been crestfallen, and I suspected that, after shedding some tears, Jenny would have felt the way I did.

Each member of the Veneziale family was so nice to us that I questioned whether they were genuinely that kind or whether pity dictated their actions.

When Mrs. V, as she asked us to call her, offered to show us how to make stuffed shells on day four because we'd both loved them, I admitted that emotions more noble than pity were at play.

Eventually, Mom returned. We heard her shouting for us from our doorway, a few doors away. We hugged everyone, thanked them for the fortieth time, then dragged ourselves home.

The reunion with Mom was as unpleasant as you'd suspect it would be, as though Jenny and I had been the ones who'd disappeared for nearly a week without explanation.

The next day she abandoned our apartment and moved us into Allen Tiedje's house in Midtown. He'd met Mom in Roof Brothers and hit it off enough that he asked her to drive to Dayton with him to deliver a package. Most people would consider that proposition unwise, at best, possibly terrifying, but not Mom. She jumped in the car, and they got along well enough that we moved in with him as soon as they returned.

Mom never knew that Mrs. V had called the Kentucky Child Abuse Reporting Hotline on day four. I later heard from a classmate who lived in our apartment complex that a man and a woman showed up at our old apartment two days after we abandoned it, looking for my mom. They probably would have taken us away.

Allen Tiedje kicked us out nine weeks later.

Those ten weeks were the most tumultuous and traumatic stretch of our childhoods, particularly because Allen believed that because we were under his roof, he had the right to hit us, too.

But that first week, the one spent in a home filled with love and laughter, was the best week of my childhood, and it showed me that I could aspire to be something more than destiny seemed to want me to be. I didn't have to put up with disfunction and abuse. I didn't have to settle for barely tolerable when the world also contains magnificence.

Sadly, it took me far longer to put that realization into action than it should have, but the Veneziales showed me it could be done. We remained friends until the twins left for college and Mr. and Mrs. V moved to Boca Raton.

Today, when I want to eat a bowl of love, I prepare Mrs. V's Stuffed Shells.

FOR THE SAUCE:
3 TBLs olive oil plus 2 TBLs
4 cloves garlic, minced
1 can tomato paste
1 large can San Marzano peeled tomatoes
1/2 an onion, finely chopped
1/2 bell pepper, diced (optional)
Italian seasoning
Salt
Pepper
Red Pepper flakes

IF YOU'D LIKE to prepare whichever sauce you usually use, now's the time to do it. Yes, you can use store-bought pasta sauce, but you can also open a can of SpaghettiOs, declare yourself the Queen of Sheba, and demand to be enshrined in the Quilters Hall of Fame.

You should not do any of these.

If you'd like to use Mrs. V's, or put your own spin on it, here's where to start:

Pour 3 tablespoons of olive oil into a large skillet on low to medium heat.

Add the garlic and onions to the pan. Let them brown before you add the tomato paste, which you should also let brown.

Add the chopped tomatoes, mash them, and blend with the paste, garlic, and onions. Add the bell pepper if you're using it. If you aren't, you probably shouldn't have diced it.

Add salt, pepper, red pepper, and Italian herbs to taste.

If you had to give away one item of clothing, which one would it be? As the pasta sauce simmers on low heat, retrieve that item of clothing and set it by the front door so you can give it away tomorrow.

For the pasta:

35 to 40 jumbo pasta shells

In a large pot, boil plenty of salted water (not a dash of salt but a handful). Add the shells to the boiling water. Cook until the pasta is al dente (the time required is probably on the package). When the shells are ready, they should be between crunchy and mushy.

Drain the water. Let the shells cool for a while. You may want to separate the shells on a cookie sheet so they don't stick together. This isn't absolutely necessary, but when you struggle later to separate the shells that seem to have glued themselves to each other, remember that this passage was here for your convenience and not because I felt like tying randomly like this dlasjbg pier JGOIKANSFGBNKLlksjdgner.

Preheat oven to 375

. . .

FOR THE FILLING:

4 cups spinach, chopped

32 ounces ricotta

1 1/2 cups mozzarella, grated

1 1/2 cups parmesan, grated

1/2 cup cheddar, grated

1/4 cup Great Value First Blend (Monterey Jack, cheddar, queso quesadilla, asadero), optional

2 eggs, beaten

1 tsp onion powder

1 1/2 tsps Italian herbs

1/2 tsp parsley

1/2 tsp basil

1 1/2 tsps salt

3/4 tsp ground pepper

IN ANOTHER LARGE frying pan on medium heat, pour two tablespoons of olive oil and maneuver it so it covers the bottom of the pan.

Add the chopped spinach and stir it gently as it wilts for about three minutes. If you wilt the spinach for 3 minutes and 22 seconds, no one will care.

Set the pan aside to cool. Yes, I understand that you have now used many pots and pans, so I hope your kitchen has plenty of surfaces and that you're not using a hot plate to prepare this meal. If you are—and you do so successfully—maybe you should write a cookbook called, Hot Plate Supreme. Or you could go with a good title.

In a large bowl, mix all of the cheeses you're choosing to use.

Add all of the spices and the eggs, then mix.

Add the spinach, then incorporate.

If you've let the shells glue themselves together, now's the time to regret not heeding my advice above.

Take out the largest casserole dish you likely own (unless you run a restaurant, in which case why are you reading *my* cookbook instead of writing your own? That may be something you should discuss with your friends and family).

Ladle sauce across the bottom.

Use a tablespoon to stuff the shells (hence the name of this dish). Set each stuffed-to-the-brim shell in the casserole dish (I used a lasagna pan for this recipe, and I didn't have enough room for all of the stuffed shells. You don't want to layer them, but you also don't want to waste them. In other words, you may need to use an additional casserole dish).

When you've snuggled the stuffed shells into the dish just so, ladle the rest of the sauce over the top. If you want to sprinkle some grated cheese on top now, no one will stop you. Well, maybe someone who's lactose intolerant, but it's a bit late in the game to introduce that obstacle to this scenario, so forget I mentioned it.

Cover the dish, pan, tray, or whatever you have placed the shells in with aluminum foil.

Bake at 375 for 25 minutes

Carefully remove the foil.

Bake for an additional 10 to 15 minutes

Remove the pan from the oven. Let cool, then enjoy.

Mrs. V encouraged Jenny and me to have a second and even a third helping. I took her up on her offer, and when I prepare Mrs. V's Stuffed Shells, I encourage my friends, family, and the occasional stranger to do the same.

NANNA GUIDREY'S SHRIMP & GRITS

Makes 4 cookbook servings
(or 2 realistic servings with a skosh left over for a midnight snack)

. . .

MIKE WEISS, after tasting my version of his family's jambalaya recipe, decided that I wouldn't bungle another of his family's recipes, so he bestowed upon me Nanna Guidry's recipe for shrimp and grits. I prepared it for him before I included it in the cookbook.

"You nailed it," he said after wiping his mouth. "I wouldn't change a thing. Now which dessert did you pair with this meal?"

"Dessert, really? This was rich enough to pass as a dessert."

"Passing as a dessert isn't the same as being one. What did you bring?"

"Biscotti."

"Can't argue with that … and I argue for a living."

FOR THE GRITS:
   3 cups whole milk
   ½ tsp salt
   1 cup quick-cooking grits
   ½ cup shredded parmesan
   1 cup shredded sharp cheddar
   1 clove of garlic, pressed
   Dash of cayenne
   Black pepper to taste
   2 TBLs butter

FOR THE SHRIMP:
   1 pound large shrimp, peeled and deveined
   If you peel them yourself, they should weigh 1 pound after peeling. If using frozen, allow them to thaw and the excess frost to drain off.
   1 3-ounce link andouille sausage, diced (Aidell's is a good, widely available brand)
   2 TBLs butter
   3 TBLs olive oil

6 cloves garlic, put through a press or finely minced by hand
½ a medium onion, diced
1 small or ½ large green bell pepper, diced
3 stalks celery, diced
½ tsp salt
¼ tsp cayenne pepper
¼ tsp black pepper
¼ tsp white pepper
1 tsp dried basil
½ tsp dried thyme
¼ tsp smoked paprika
1 TBL Worchestershire sauce
1 bay leaf
½ cup cooking liquid (chicken stock, beer, or dry white wine—
cook's choice)

FOR THE CRISPY OKRA TOPPING:
**1 pound fresh or 12 ounces frozen okra, cut into 1/2-inch thick
chunks**
2 TBLs high smoke point cooking oil (corn, canola, safflower)
Salt and pepper to taste

IN A LARGE, heavy skillet, brown the diced andouille in the butter and olive oil over medium-high heat. You want it to get nicely browned with crisp edges. Add the garlic, diced vegetables, salt and spices. Turn the burner down to a low setting and cook the mixture until the vegetables begin to brown and slightly caramelize, about 10 minutes.

While the vegetables do their thing, ask yourself: If I had to live within any one sitcom in television history, which one would I step into, and how long would it take before my family knew I was gone?

Once you've answered those questions to your satisfaction, you can move the skillet to the back burner if needed while you prepare the grits and the rest of the meal.

For the grits, bring the milk and salt to a boil, then add the grits. Cover and simmer on low heat for about 5 minutes, then stir in the cheeses, butter, garlic, cayenne, and black pepper. Turn off the heat, put the lid on, and hold until the rest of the meal is finished.

Was it *Gilligan's Island? Happy Days? Bewitched?*

Please tell me it wasn't *Alf.*

In a mixing bowl, toss the cut okra, cooking oil, salt, and pepper. Spread on a cookie sheet and **roast in an oven set to 425 until crispy and brown, about 15 minutes.**

Stir a couple of times during the roasting. When the okra is crisp, turn the oven off and set aside until the rest of the meal is ready.

When it is almost time to eat, bring the skillet back to a sizzle over medium-high heat and add the cooking liquid and Worchestershire.

Bring to a rolling boil and add the shrimp. Cook the shrimp in the sauce just long enough to turn them pink and opaque. The sauce should be rich, thick, and of just enough volume to coat the shrimp and veggies. If there was too much water in the shrimp, you can rescue the sauce by removing the shrimp, cooking down the sauce for a couple of minutes, then re-adding the shrimp.

Remove the bay leaf. Remove from heat and serve immediately.

To plate the dish, put about a cup of grits on a plate, spoon the shrimp around the grits, spoon sauce over the grits, and garnish with ¼ cup of the crispy okra.

Yes, this dish is ambitious, but it is definitely worth the effort—especially if all you have to do is wait to eat while someone else prepares it.

NOT JUST ANOTHER KALE SALAD, & LIVELY LEMON DRESSING

*S*erves 2 or 3

. . .

I EAT MORE salads than the average American, and certainly more than the average resident of the Republic of Ireland. A vegan friend of mine visited Dublin recently and told me after she returned that when she'd asked for a salad in a pub, the male server said, "You're in the wrong place, love. Get along now." In a restaurant, an angry server summoned the chef who told her, "Ya want a salad, do you? Paid to fly here so you could avoid eating the local cuisine, is that it? Too good for everything that's on my menu, are you? What if I do this for you, dearie: What if I give you a shepherd's pie, and you call it what you want? Shepard's salad? Fine with me. Do we have a deal?"

A bit hostile, I'd say.

And I'm sure many of you feel a bit hostile toward me because I've written a cookbook that doesn't include a single dish in which bacon is the star. Fair point, but those cookbooks exist by the hundreds, so I don't need to add to that collection. After all, most of the dishes I've included will clog your arteries just as well as bacon will.

But this isn't one of them.

LIVELY LEMON and Olive Oil Salad Dressing

6 TBLs olive oil

1 tsp freshly ground black pepper (15 turns of my pepper grinder. I've never used yours, so I'll defer to you.)

½ tsp sea salt

1 large clove garlic

Juice of 1 large lemon

¼ tsp red pepper flakes

¼ cup freshly grated parmesan

1/8 cup plain bread crumbs

3/4 cup cherry, grape, or other small tomatoes, halved

Kale (preferably lacinato, but regular kale will work as long as it is not the pre-chopped kind—that way lies madness), **spinach, spring**

mix, or any mixture thereof, enough to make 6 cups after thinly slicing into a chiffonade.

If you're pretty sure you can't stand kale and wish it didn't exist so you never have to hear people prattle on about their kale smoothies and how they may name their next child, regardless of gender, Kale, try making this salad with the midrib removed and the kale leaves thinly sliced as directed. You will likely change your mind.

However, if you don't, you can frivolously sue me, but I never told you to buy this cookbook or to make this salad or to harbor an inexplicable animosity toward a leafy vegetable.

Dressing:

Juice the lemon into a large mixing bowl.

Put the garlic clove through a press and mix with the lemon juice.

Add the black pepper, red pepper flakes, and salt, then whisk briefly.

Add the olive oil, and whisk rapidly. The mixture should form a thick emulsion pretty easily.

Meanwhile, prepare the greens. If you are using kale, first wash it thoroughly. Next, remove the tough midrib from each leaf.

Chiffonade the greens (slice thinly with a sharp chef's knife). For lacinato kale, it is efficient to stack the leaves and slice through the whole stack. These thin slices make the difference between a tough kale salad that is unpleasant to eat and a tender kale salad that bursts with flavor. For spinach or spring mix, you don't have to do a superfine chiffonade, but at least slice them so there aren't any huge leaves in the salad.

If the greens had to be washed (meaning, if you used kale), either blot them dry thoroughly with a kitchen towel or put them through a salad spinner to dry.

What is the square root of 81?

You should know this one. It's not that difficult. I know it's been a long time since you took a math class, but still …

Which two identical numbers multiplied together give you 81?

End of the mathematical interlude. Be on the lookout for history questions. You may want to brush up on the Tea Pot Dome scandal and the Archduke Ferdinand.

Toss the greens and the tomato in the dressing.

Just before serving, sprinkle the parmesan and breadcrumbs on the salad and toss some more.

The breadcrumbs help distribute the dressing, and also make the salad a little more filling, in a way that is much easier to eat than croutons.

9

The answer is nine.

But you knew that.

This salad is addictive and adaptable. For a low-ish carb, high-protein meal, top a large bowl of this with a chunk of broiled salmon, grilled chicken, or sautéed shrimp. It can make a nice starting course for a formal meal, but it can also be a side dish on a disposable plate at a picnic.

If you use kale, the salad will still be good the next day.

The Tea Pot Dome scandal involved the Warren G. Harding administration, bribery, and the Secretary of the Interior, whose name was—I kid you not—Albert Bacon Fall. He was sentenced to prison, where I'm certain he wasn't served even the most boring, run-of-the-mill kale salad, let alone the one you can now make whenever you want to do so, provided you didn't stop reading when I used the word chiffonade.

PASTA AND GARBONZOS

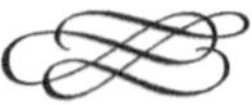

*M*akes 4 servings

. . .

You may know them as chickpeas, garbanzo beans, or Egyptian peas, but unless you're a botanist or a true legume fanatic, you probably didn't know that their scientific name is *Cicer arietinum*.

Now that you know that, you may want to forget it because knowing Latin, or even just one two-word phrase of it (with the possible exception of *caveat emptor*) will not help you while following this recipe.

I'll vouch for this meal's deliciousness but won't take credit for its creation because it came to me in a dream, much the way that Paul McCartney had the beautiful, heart-rending ballad *Yesterday* come to him while he slept. But the dream part is where the similarity ends. He's made millions in royalties, but I get to enjoy this meal whenever I want. Of course, now that I've written this book, so can he (if he buys a copy; I'm not about to give a free book to a billionaire—unless he chooses to promote it, of course. Heck, I'd rename it in that case. *Hey Jude, Wanna Bake?* Or *Let It Be Delicious!* Anyone know how to reach Sir Paul?).

Regardless of whether Mr. McCartney decides to lend his name to this effort, I'd like to thank him for creating *Yesterday* and all of the other masterpieces he's created and performed. For the record, I prepared the following meal while listening to *Abbey Road*. Talk about a win-win!

3 TBLs olive oil
> **1 medium onion, chopped**
> **1 carrot or a handful of baby carrots, chopped**
> **2 garlic cloves, minced**
> **1 rounded teaspoon of salt**
> **Black pepper, plenty of it**
> **Red pepper flakes, to taste.** A pinch for wimps; a dash for ho-hum middle-of-the-roaders; and a dash and a half or even two for people who believe in all that is right and true
> **1 sprig of fresh rosemary, finely chopped**
> **1 bay leaf**

1 28-ounce can of San Marzano tomatoes, crushed

2 cups of chicken broth, bone broth, vegetable broth, or Fruit Juicy Red flavored Hawaiian Punch (just making sure you're paying attention. I've made this dish with the first three, and I enjoyed them all. I don't recommend using any flavor of Hawaiian Punch in this dish. For legal reasons I cannot disparage this product or any that features large amounts of high fructose corn syrup or FD&C Red 40, a dye made in part from petroleum).

In other words, go with one of the broths.

1 can of chickpeas or garbanzo beans, including the liquid, which is called aquafaba.

1 ½ cups cellentani pasta or another pasta of your choice that isn't spaghetti, linguini, vermicelli, capellini (angel hair) or the like. By the way, according to the Pasta Shapes Dictionary, more than 600 pasta shapes exist. Don't lose sleep if you can't name more than a dozen. If you can name more than 30, you're not spending enough time quilting.

Chopped fresh parsley

On a medium setting, heat the olive oil in a large saucepan (I use a Dutch oven, which people in the Netherlands would call a braadpan, although they wouldn't be referring to the same kind of pot. I had a Dutch roommate in college, and she wouldn't eat this dish because she didn't like garlic. She did like Hawaiian Punch, though. She's dead.).

Using the back of your knife, push the onion and carrots from the cutting board into whichever kind of pot you're using. Cook until the carrots are softened, approximately 10 minutes, stirring every so often.

Add rosemary, salt, and garlic, then stir for about 1 minute (or 60 seconds if you prefer your minutes in minute increments).

Stir in broth, chickpeas, including aquafaba, the entire contents of the tomato can, bay leaf, red pepper flakes, and chopped rosemary.

This step isn't necessary (but then, neither is making this dish, if you really think about it, which I don't suggest you do because you're probably hungry, and contemplating the merits of a particular dish has never filled a stomach), but if you feel inclined to do so, as I did, then scoop one cup of the mixture in the pot into a blender or some other high-speed whirling device (not a fan), then blend on high for fifteen seconds. Return the blended mixture to the pot, then **bring it all to a boil.**

Stir in the pasta of your choice, except the kinds listed above.

Cook for 12 minutes on medium heat.

Check to see if the pasta is al dente, Italian for "to the tooth," which I translate as "NOT MUSHY." If you prefer your pasta to be the consistency of baby food, well, bless your heart.

Fish out the bay leaf, then taste the HOT dish to see if you'd like to add salt, pepper, or more red pepper flakes. Ladle the steamy goodness into bowls, sprinkle on the parsley, and enjoy.

ROASTED BEETS AND SWEET POTATOES

*S*erves 5

. . .

AFTER MY STINT in the CIA, I decided to become a juggler of violins. The money turned out to be less than the handbook promised, and keeping the violins in tune proved to be impossible, but the overwhelming support my worldwide fanbase showered upon me was enough to sustain my lifestyle through the lean years ...

No.

After winning Best of Show at QuiltWeek Paducah for my quilted rendering of this cookbook, replete with aromatic smell-o-rama, I was offered a quilting ambassadorship to Madagascar and granted unlimited quantities of vanilla.

No.

How about:

This beets and sweet potatoes dish bathed in pomegranate molasses delivers plenty of flavor and antioxidants, without the need for covert operations.

On the other hand, what better cover story for a spy than to be an award-winning quilter and an unassuming ambassador who sources locally grown vanilla for her baked goods while secretly plotting to overthrow the empire of Martha Stewart?

No.

PREHEAT OVEN **to 400**

3 cups beets, peeled and cubed, 2-3 large beets

1 large sweet potato

3 TBLs olive oil

4 TBLs pomegranate molasses, a tart syrup of pomegranates available at Middle Eastern or international markets. If unavailable, a good substitute is 3 TBLs balsamic vinegar mixed with 1 TBL honey.

Salt and pepper to taste

PEEL the beets and the sweet potato.

Cut into cubes with sides of about 3/4 inch.

In a large bowl, toss the cubes with the oil, salt, and pepper.

Roast at 400 until the vegetables have passed tender and are starting to carmelize, between 30 and 40 minutes.

Add either the pomegranate molasses or the balsamic/honey mixture, and roast about 10 more minutes. Watch carefully so the glaze doesn't burn.

Remove from the oven, let cool enough for you to indulge safely, then dig in.

But you knew that. You've likely been eating on your own for a while. On the other hand, people burn themselves with hot coffee then sue the restaurant that sold them the coffee because hot coffee isn't actually meant to be hot, apparently.

So, in an abundance of caution, I'm officially advising you not to scald your tongue by tasting really hot food, not to poke yourself in the eye with a sharp stick, and not to get involved in a land war in Asia unless you've worked up an immunity to iocane powder.

Or something like that.

ACKNOWLEDGMENTS

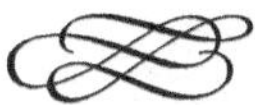

ruce here.

I'D LIKE to thank all of the thousands of readers who purchased the Hadley Carroll Mysteries. Without your support and belief in my writing, I wouldn't have written *Quilt City Cookbook*.

I couldn't have written the Hadley Carroll Mysteries or this book without the support of Paducah. Its stellar arts scene inspired the creation of Hadley and *Quilt City Murders*, and informed *Quilt City: Panic in Paducah*. I will, therefore, forever be grateful to the residents of Paducah and to the institutions and businesses there that have shown tremendous support for me, namely the National Quilt Museum, With Love, From Kentucky, the Yeiser Art Center, and JCCB Vendors.

Thank you to Rob Samborn, Shanessa Gluhm, Alex Blevens, Ty Keenum, Laurel Kile, and Ruthie Marlenée for encouraging me to turn a whacky idea into a cookbook. And I'd like to thank Bonnie K. Hunter for her promotional savvy and her generosity.

I owe an immeasurable debt to my mother, Barbara Leonard, who taught me how to bake and suggested that I always "double the vanilla," no matter how much a recipe specifies. I don't suggest you do that with these recipes because I've already done it.

Nearly all of the savory recipes in this cookbook came from the creative mind of my wife, Sedonia Sipes, who cooks so well that I don't like going out to dinner because the quality of the meals in restaurants is nearly always a step or two below her delicious creations.

If you enjoyed reading this cookbook and have found some of the recipes to be worthy of five stars, please leave a rating and/or a review on whichever platform you prefer.

I'll keep you informed about the latest Hadley developments—publication dates, book signings, giveaways—if you sign up for my newsletter on my website: https://bruceleonardwriter.com

Thank you for your support and for your continued membership on Team Hadley.

HADLEY HERE.

I'M IN LITERARY LIMBO, Bruce.

Sure, I've enjoyed writing this cookbook, despite the pounds I put on while doing so, but I'm the namesake of the Hadley Carroll Mysteries, emphasis on *mysteries*.

So far in this award-winning series, the mysteries have had me racing around non-stop, yet all I'm doing now is twiddling my thumbs and downing Magnificent Mocha Panna Cotta instead of investigating leads, pursuing justice, gathering clues, delving into malfeasance, prodding close-lipped officials for comments about corruption, and tracking down murderers.

In other words, I want to get back to work.

Kill somebody already.

PRAISE FOR THE HADLEY CARROLL MYSTERIES

*uilt City: Panic in Paducah* is "Better than *Quilt City Murders,* and I LOVED that novel."
— Jenny Raith, <u>CozyMysteryBookshop.com</u>

"HADLEY CARROLL IS BACK! The intrepid, wisecracking quilter-reporter is on the scene in this cozy mystery that starts with a bang, hooks you in, and doesn't let go. Filled with wit, nuggets of wisdom, and twists you won't see coming, *Quilt City: Panic in Paducah* is the perfect second installment in the Hadley Carroll Mystery Series. A must read!"
— Rob Samborn, author of *The Prisoner of Paradise*

"THE FIRST BOOK in this series was great—this one was even better." — an Amazon reviewer

AS THE FABRIC OF PADUCAH, Kentucky, begins to unravel again with a string of crimes and murders, veteran investigative journalist Hadley

Carroll and her new love interest Brandon Green begin to iron out the town's problems and restore order. Author Bruce Leonard cuts on the bias, does not miss a stitch, and delivers this fast-paced who-done-it with smooth prose, wit, and just the right amount of sarcastic color. Grab some cookies and hot chocolate, wrap yourself in a warm quilt, and enjoy this cozy mystery; you'll be happy you did.

— Alex Blevens, author of *Bycatch*

I BEGAN READING this book and was drawn right in. I had a hard time putting it down to sleep at night. Well written and kept me interested. Hadley Carroll is a very interesting character. Looking forward to the next book. — an Amazon reviewer

READING *QUILT CITY: Panic in Paducah* was an absolute treat. Bruce Leonard strikes the perfect blend of humor and mystery in this gripping sequel that is somehow even better than its predecessor.

Fast, fun, and unputdownable, five stars is not nearly enough. I'm hooked on Hadley!

— Shanessa Gluhm, author of *Enemies of Doves*

HADLEY'S THOUGHTS and speech are littered with bon mots that will have you laughing out loud. The witticisms give a break from the tense twists and turns of the plot, and the reader is kept guessing right up until the end. I'm looking forward to Leonard's next release.

— Ty Keenum, author of *The Little Church in the Valley*

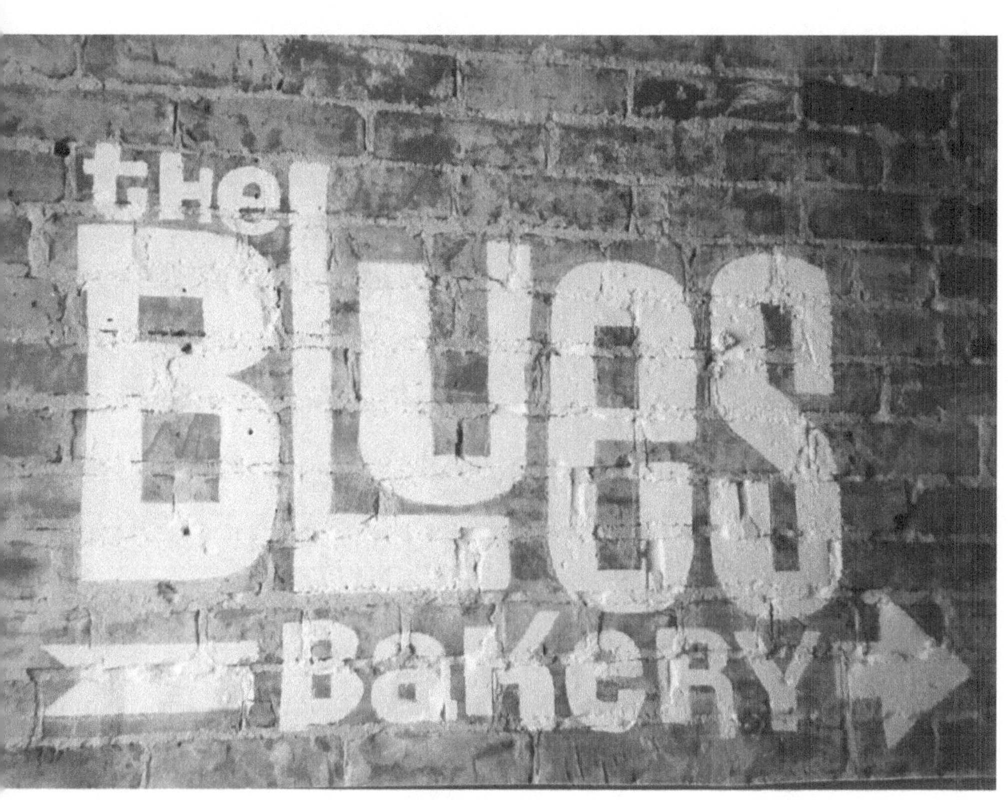

tHe
BLUes
BaKeRY

ABOUT THE AUTHOR

Bruce Leonard earned a B.A. in English with a creative-writing emphasis from UCLA. He has been a travel writer, a magazine- and newspaper editor, an owner of a bakery, and a guinea pig for the U.S. Government.

He writes the award-winning, bestselling Hadley Carroll Mysteries, the first of which, Quilt City Murders, was named Best Mystery of 2022 in one contest. The fifth installment will be titled, Quilt City: Safety Second.

The first Jack Drake Private-Eye Mystery, Hard Exit, narrated by a depressed private investigator to the stars in Malibu, is available now at the above link, or at https://a.co/d/2Q71oQP, if you're reading this in paperback. The sequel will be Stronger at the Break.

Quilt City Murders, the first Hadley Carroll Mystery, named Best Mystery of 2022 by the National Indie Excellence Awards

Quilt City: Panic in Paducah, the second

Quilt City: Measure Once, Cut Twice, the third

Quilt City: Proving a Negative, the fourth

Quilt City Cookbook, a companion book narrated by Hadley at her funniest and most vulnerable

Bruce's website is: https://bruceleonardwriter.com/, where his books are available. While there, please sign up for his infrequent newsletter, in which he keeps readers informed about upcoming releases, and you can look at a smattering of the thousands of photos he took when he was a travel writer.

Happy reading!